HEART DOG

Gunner's Story

KAREN GRZENDA

Cover Design: Karen Grzenda

Photo credits:
Professional Dog Show Pictures - Faye Unrau Photography

Cover picture of Gunner and Karen - Eileen Bennett

DEDICATION

"People and dogs come into your life for a reason, a season or a lifetime"

I'd like to dedicate this book to the following people:

My dearest love Tim: Thank you so much for your patience, kindness and all the support you've given me in this endeavor. With you, all my hopes and dreams are become reality!

To my primary editors Aunty Dee and Aunty Eileen: I will never forget all the love, support and hard work you've both put into making this book come true!

To my Mom and Dad: I love you both so much! Every day I wrote, I sat in dad's chair with the beautiful view of the water inspiring me.

Pat, Mandy, Michele, Donna, Uncle Frank, Johnny, Dawn, Dolly and Jake

Contents

Contents

ACKNOWLEDGMENTS

Dog Show People: Tracy (Dobes), Carol (Rotties), Cindy (Dobes and Min Pins), Geri (Boxers), Jillian (Goldens), Ed (Rotties), Jim (Boxers), Joan (Pugs/Chins), Lynda (Dobes), Christine (Whippets), Irenne (Corgis), Katherina (Briards and Salukis), Susan (Bassets), Trina (Bassets), Kara (Border Collies), Lu (GSD's), Pearl (Terriers), Lisa (Collies, Italian Greyhounds etc.), Claudia (Shelties), Linda and Larry (Wheatens), Maureen (Aussies and Corgis), Shauna (Aussies), Angel, Janice (Vislas) and so many more whom touched our lives.

Blue Doberman / Rescue Doberman Email List: Please keep sharing your stories, offering input and knowledge. Your guidance, support and prayers save lives! Rusty, Bug, Deb, Eliz, Gypsieman, Becca, Aunty Caroline, Marci, Carol, Lee Ann, Paul, Elaine, Ceilidh, Margaret, Mary, Dawn, Judy, Betsy, and all the other list members whom ever offered input.

Never Forgotten
"Aunty" Shirley Shaski and Chrisy (Rotties)

To all our beloved canine friends waiting at the bridge for us!

The Canine Thyroid Epidemic
Authors: W. Jean Dodds, DVM and Diana R. Laverdure

INTRODUCTION

I've spent years thinking about writing this book and didn't because of pile of different fears. Fear of failure, fear of "doing it wrong" and not telling the "right" story. Fear of butchering this book and in turn doing a "disservice" to all the dogs who've come and gone in my life.

Nowadays, you can go online and see a book and before you buy it, read all the positive and nasty "feedback" that people leave in the comments and decide if you even want to open the cover. The fear of judgement by others is there as well as is the fear that all my "if I would have", "maybe I could have", or the worst, "I should have" will come back.

That fear of failure is minimal to the fear I have of talking about our Gunner and having people condemn him and his breed and not seeing that this could and probably has happened to so many others and so many breeds.

But my biggest fear out of all my fears is that another dog will live in pain like Gunner did because I didn't have the guts to tell his story and share what I have learned. Or worse, a dog will be put down without knowing the true story of his or her "why?"

If you've gotten this far, I implore you to read this book before you judge. See more than a breed, see that this can happen to anyone, even people whom think they "know it all".

Please read this book and learn from my mistakes. Share this book and maybe even save a life whether it's animal or human.

And truly, although this seems like just another "dog book" just for dog people, this is actually a "living being" book for all people. The most valuable lesson Gunner taught me was that when you "know" something is wrong with someone you love, you never stop fighting to find out! You are your own, and the ones you love, advocate. Doctors and vets go to school and there is no denying that they know stuff, lots of stuff, but if you live with someone who has "something wrong" and are consistently told the opposite, you owe it to your loved one to find out for sure.

You know them. Please fight for them.

1 ~ TO ALL THE DOGS I'VE LOVED BEFORE

My love for dogs started many years ago, at the wee age of two.

Often in a little red coat, I spent time with two St. Bernards named Govenor and Dutchess who lived across the street from us in Winnipeg, Manitoba, Canada. I don't remember much of that time but I'm told that mom and dad had difficulties dragging me away from them and them from me. I vaguely remember them, I guess because I was so little, but I do remember slobber, kindness, and a weird sense of peace.

Sadly when I was about four years old, those big, fluffy, slobbering canine babysitters moved. This left me alone nursing my first dog heartbreak.

My gramma said that in my grief, I "found" other dogs and brought them home to mom begging that I be able to keep them. The "found" part was a reach as they usually had leashes and collars attached to them. I never got to keep any of them and to this day I don't remember this time but I want to apologize to anyone who had their beloved pet stolen forty some odd years ago by a little four year old. But I guess we all do what we have to do.

Rusty came as basically a threat from my Gramma and God bless her for that. My understanding of the events is that Gramma set a timeline for mom and dad to get me a dog as my childhood thievery simply couldn't go on. If they failed to meet this timeline, Gramma would find my new friend and it would be a St. Bernard because of my connection to Govenor and Dutchess.

I believe to this day that St. Bernards are amazing dogs but as with any breed, they truly need to fit the family. From what I understand, mom started investigating breeds and even took me to a variety of breeders as she was quite certain that the lovely St. Bernard breed just wasn't a good fit for our family at that time.

The story that has been told over and over at family dinners is how it became painfully obvious to mom that during our search for my next best friend, Pugs would prove to not be my particular breed of choice.

I take this time to apologize to Pug owners as they, like the St. Bernards, are amazing dogs that fit perfectly with certain families, but for me at four, apparently not ours. Where I applaud my mom for doing her due diligence and taking the time to investigate various breeds, I clearly and quickly let her know that Pugs did not fit our family and were not my breed of choice.

Mom says I was excited, so terribly excited to go see puppies so we were definitely off to a good start! We got out of the car at the breeders home and this precious little pug came running down the walkway to great us with such enthusiasm and excitement. I took one look, screamed for my life and literally climbed my mother in fear. Again, I'm sorry to pug people but that was the deciding factor right there that a pug would not be in our family.

The next visit to breeders I do somewhat remember. This is where I found my new best friend in a gorgeous yellow Labrador that soon became my Rusty!

I remember going into the house and immediately seeing the momma dog behind a baby gate wagging her tail at us and smiling with her tongue hanging out of the side of her mouth.

We went downstairs to the most magical place ever! There was a very large box, not very high but there were bright yellow puppies everywhere! I know this can't be fact, but I guess with childhood excitement, it seemed like hundreds, thousands, maybe even millions of them!

I don't remember if I asked, or if I was told, if someone put me in, or if I jumped in by my own self, but I just remember all of a sudden being in that box covered with puppies! As I write this, 40 some odd years later, I feel a warmth in my heart as I type and have happy tears in my eyes.

They were so beautiful and they barked, licked and just surrounded me with love! Mom said I grabbed hold of one and while she squirmed, squished in my four year old little arms, it was confirmed by the breeder she was a girl and immediately she was mine! I named her right there in that box; in my arms was my new best friend Rusty!

Interestingly enough, mom told me later that as is quite common with breeders, each of those puppies had been tattooed and already given registered names. When the tattoo was checked, my new best friend Rusty had the registered name of "Trusious Golden Rusty". So I guess the old saying "it was meant to be" comes into play here.

Throughout the years, Rusty and I grew incredibly close as best friends do.

She let me dress her up in mom's old maternity clothes and we went for walks down the street like princesses!

We baked mud pies together out in the back yard with her water dish as the pan and the garden hose providing the "mix".

Every day before school in the morning after Aunty Mildred called me for wake up, we'd head down into the basement where she laid on the chair and watched me roller skate tiny laps in the basement.

We had countless tea parties and even ran away together because we were mad at mom, down the street to my other friends' house, a human named Kim. We only lasted a few hours "on the lam" before Kim's mom sent us home but Rusty and I had made our point with mom.

One of our favorite past times was climbing our crab apple tree and true to form, Rusty was always supportive. I remember her sitting or lying down at the bottom of the tree just waiting ever so patiently. She was such a good dog. It probably helped her decision to stay as I would throw down the occasional ripe apple to her.

Rusty trusted me, she was patient and kind even when, as a child, I wasn't.

I think it's true, dogs do teach you things that you can't learn from humans. Maybe because when you get things wrong, they don't tell you that you got it wrong. They don't condemn you for making mistakes as some people do. They let you realize it for yourself and isn't that the best way to really learn lessons?

The first hard lesson for me was learning not to leave toys laying around. Sadly, I lost my best friend Rusty after she chewed up one of my homemade Barbie couches and a nail lodged in her throat. Fortunately for me, or maybe not, I was sleeping over at Gramma's house and didn't have to see this first hand. Mom and dad took Rusty to the vet but she couldn't be saved and I never had the chance to say "Good bye" to my best friend. Often, throughout the years, I've still felt that guilt, still held onto the fact that my best friend died because I was careless.

I stayed at Gramma's that night, and I do remember crying so hard and so deep and being so completely sure that it was all a mistake or maybe even a lie. At one point while lying in Grammas bed in her cozy warm flannel pajamas, I swore I could hear Rusty's toe nails clicking on the floor. I think I was eight or nine at that time but believe me, it's stuck with me and is something I'll never forget. I think she came to say goodbye.

Since Rusty, I've been blessed with so many dogs.

"Blackie" was some sort of black lab/shepherd cross that I found terrified on the hood of a car in a Zellers parking lot. I'm not sure what his story was but I know now he was obviously miss-treated as he was very aggressive. It took me hours to coax him into a rope and finally get him home. I can't remember how long we had him but he did bite me and mom decided to take him to the pound. I don't blame her, and I don't blame him, I just pray someone took him and loved him.

"Snowball" was an amazing little Bichon Frise that dad bought from a pet store for me when I was about twelve. He loved to swim with me and quite commonly got snagged in bushes which we tromped through on hikes at our cottage in Ontario.

Snowball had a big dog personality and had no problems taking on Trapper, a black lab who after being neutered started trying to mount him. Snowball, being a quarter of this dogs size, got angry and with a great Bichon ninja leap, grabbed hold of Trapper's nose and hung there until he fell off. Trapper never bothered little Snowball again! Not only that, but Trapper had scars on his nose for years to come after that altercation.

Snowball loved it when I had summer break from school but peed on my bed for weeks after I returned to classes, leaving him by himself. Together, he and I had to be treated for duck lice caused by investigating the death of a Canada goose with a stick at Oak Hammock Marsh. Snowball and I "hung out" and he helped me grow into my teen years. He listened to my problems and he was there for me when I needed him and again, my friend.

"Trapper" that black lab previously mentioned, adopted me as his "summer owner" at our cottage in LacLu, Ontario. Trapper's owner Brian worked night shifts and so when Brian came home in the early morning, he'd put Trapper out loose so he could sleep. Trapper would come directly to our cottage and hang out with me until he had to go in at night for Brian's nightshift.

Trapper and I also became very close as we spent a lot of time doing exactly what Labradors love to do most and that was swimming. The hours we spent on the dock either swimming together or fishing was incredible. If I was fishing, I was also throwing the stick constantly for Trapper.

One evening while driving home with Trapper loose in the bed of his truck, Brian was hit head on by a drunk driver. Brian was seriously injured but Trapper was also thrown from the bed of his truck.

Two days later, with a broken leg, broken arm and multiple broken ribs, Brian came to our cottage and asked mom if he could take me to help him find Trapper.

We went back to the crash site and while Brain drove slowly, I walked up and down for approximately a mile stretch calling Trapper's name the whole time and doing my classic hand clapping. I was only about thirteen or fourteen at the time and the way Brian explained it, Trapper was a hunting dog that retrieved fowl but also displayed strong tracking instincts. It was Brain's hope that Trapper would come across my scent and stick by it.

We didn't find Trapper that day but a few days later, Brain got a call from a person saying that there was a crazy black dog running up and down the highway and he wouldn't come to anyone. Immediately Brian came and again requested my assistance.

I'll never forget it. We got to the crash site and sure enough Trapper was running on the shoulder away from us. Before Brian could bring the truck to a complete stop, I jumped out and with blurred vision from all my tears, I started clapping and calling Trapper. He stopped dead in his tracks, spun around and I swear, I'd never seen him move that fast!

Trapper completely bowled me over and the two of us rolled on the gravel shoulder in a tight embrace with me crying and him covering me in kisses. Brian still could barely walk so after Trapper and I finished our "smooch fest", I had him jump into the truck where he covered Brian in kisses too.

Fortunately, after the vet visit, it was determined that Trapper had come out of the accident very lucky and had no injuries. It was the vets' opinion that maybe when he was thrown from the truck, instead of hitting pavement, he hit the marshy ditch. It was likely that he went into shock for a number of days and then found my scent on the road as Brian said he would.

Trapper was so stinky and thin that it was hard to believe he was even Trapper!

Brian again requested my assistance, this time in taking Trapper for a quick swim to clean him off and then even asked if Trapper could sleep over at our cottage for the next little while as Brian wasn't in any condition to take care of Trapper. Of course I eagerly agreed, mom didn't mind and even Snowball seemed to understand!

Trapper and I had an amazing summer love for many years until sadly one year I got to the cottage and called my Trapper and he didn't come. I finally went down to Brians' house and that's when he told me he had to put Trapper down due to severe arthritis. Again my heart was broken.

"Sasha" was a gorgeous, yellow lab/Samoyed cross who was given to me by a neighbor before being tossed in the river for not looking like a purebred lab. I don't know how old she was but she could barely walk and I was young and had little knowledge of dogs at that time. With feedings every four hours and help from my Gramma, she did real well and I rehomed her when I thought she was old enough. I know now, she should have been vetted, and maybe more done for her but again, I was young and that was back in the day when a lot of dogs ran loose, didn't see vets often or at all and it was completely acceptable. I cried when I rehomed her and wonder to this day what she became and how her life played out.

"Taxi" was a crazy terrier cross approximately the size of a large loaf of bread that I actually ran over in a taxi while going to work one morning. I had her for almost fourteen years and given she was aged at two or three by the vet when I found her, that means she had a long, good life.

For those that don't know terriers, they're little scrappers and have quite the hunting instincts! When I lived in the city, she was the sweetest, kindest, snuggliest, and most kissable dog I'd ever had! Then I moved to the country and her terrier hunting side came out true to form. The first time she ever tried to kiss me with a bird leg stuck in her whiskers was the last time we kissed!

Taxi was an amazing frog, bird, mouse and vole catcher who seemed to have a three body daily limit. Any time she exceeded killing and eating three of anything in one day, I found myself holding back her hairy ears while she vomited up her kill on the carpet. She was such a good hunter in fact, that during the spring, summer and fall months I had to significantly reduce her food as she put on so much weight.

As you'll find out in this book, later in life I got quite involved in rescue dogs. I didn't do this intentionally but names get around in small communities and my community became the "dog community". I was known to take "hard cases" and handled them pretty well. I can say to this day, there's not been many dogs that scared me in my years.

Where most of the time, I was called in by various people to deal with large breed dogs and particularly Dobermans in rescue, but I also had occasion to deal with the odd small breeds.

"Bitchy", as I named her lovingly, was the one of three dogs that I ever incurred bites from and because of that, I'll never forget her.

I was called in by a relative to try to re-locate her as her family unit had fallen apart. The mother had left the father and children to run off with some guy. The father was completely broken and in his emotional state, it seemed everything in his life was in tatters.

The father had determined that the dog had to go, I think that this was primarily due to the fact that Bitchy was closest to the wife.

I agreed to go over and survey the situation and what I found was deplorable.

As was the case I experienced in many rescues, when the door was answered, I was welcomed into complete chaos. It was obvious that the father was in depression and barely living through his devastation, as the home stunk to high heaven with rotted food strewn about. The floor was covered in feces and as I was welcomed with the stench, I was also welcomed with swarming flies.

As I stood in the front doorway, and proceeded to talk to the father, I watched, Bitchy, a matted, small Lhaso Apso/Terrier cross, jump onto the couch and in plain view urinate on their furniture. It was obvious to me that this was now a habit which also explained the feces all over the floor.

She was actually quite friendly and did approach me on numerous occasions to investigate me. I simply crouched down and without making eye contact I extended my hand to her for her to sniff. I didn't push myself on her but also showed no intimidation when she barked at me from time to time. She didn't seem fearful but she was obviously cautious and not doing mentally well in the current situation which wasn't surprising.

The father agreed to let her go as did the teenage daughter and with that, they put on her leash and collar for me.

Bitchy and I left the house and proceeded to my Ford Escape which was housed with a kennel in the back for just this occasion.

Dog rescue is a funny thing. You get used to a variety of scenarios. I always found that typically even though dogs put on a mean display, usually when they were removed from the situation, they became almost thankful. I found that as long as I was cautious in the first introduction, and initial first few minutes, the rescue turned out pretty well and relaxed. But I do believe that one can become complacent to these situations as I was and as I said, I dealt with typically large breed dogs. I guess with the large breeds, I was more cautious as I felt that they could be more dangerous.

As I got Bitchy to the truck, it was obvious she was too little to jump in so I bent over to pick her up. I didn't make a fast move, nor was I standing over her per se but either way, in that moment she lunged at my hand and latched on like a pitbull!

For a little girl, man alive did she have strength in her tiny jaws!

As I write, I sigh in shame. I got my butt kicked by a little Lhaso Apso Terrier cross and my pride to this day hurts as I see the scar still on my left hand.

Eventually, I did get her to let go of me and got her into the kennel. As I sat in the front seat of the Escape mortified at the amount of blood oozing from my wounds, I remember thinking, "Unbelievable! Dobermans, Rottweilers, Pitbulls and a damn Lhaso Apso Terrier gets me". I was so embarrassed!

I was much more cautious removing her from said kennel when we arrived at the Rescue intake home and she never tagged me again. But as I told them the scenario and about the situation surrounding the bite, I felt shame as they laughed at me.

The rescue of course recommended a hospital visit and so forth but I just went home, cleaned up my wounds and circled them with felt marker to watch for infection.

The home that Bitchy came from was at one point a loving home, she had been vetted regularly as well as groomed so I didn't worry for any serious infections. I knew enough to keep things clean and watch.

Bitchy's name was changed to something like "Cutie Pie" for adoption and she did end up being moved into a wonderful home where she ended up having a wonderful life. And that's why some do rescue!

Over the years, as I have said, I've had many dogs and learned something from every one of them. Tim has said to me that people come into your lives for a reason, a season or a lifetime. I think our canine friends do the same. I still hold them all dear in my heart and all of them were precious in some way. If you're a "dog person" you get what I'm saying. If you're not a dog person then you've probably read too much of this book already as you won't "get" the rest of this journey that I'm going to try to take you on.

This journey, this book, this whatever you want to call it, is very important to me. And you may not know it yet, but if you're a dog person or close to being a dog person, it's also important to you.

See here's the thing, I've had many dogs. I've done basic doggy school and various forms of dog training including puppy class, obedience, rally, tracking and even Schutzhund. I thought I knew it all about dogs and I mean that. If you ask anyone who knows me, to this day they're shocked I never became a vet or involved in dog training professionally. I write this book because when I really thought I knew it all, along came Gunner and then I learned the most important lesson ever.

I write this book because you can never think you know it all. Always keep your mind open and always be eager to learn more. If you don't, you waste time, precious time that you may need and will no longer have.

This book has stuff that you need to learn so that it never happens again and Gunner's life with us means even more. If you take time and read this book, open your heart, and really take it all in, I promise you will learn something you didn't know.

Above : Isaac at approximately 2 years old out in Ontario.
Below : Karen and Isaac (Isaac aged at approximately 13
years old.

2 ~ ISAAC

I didn't mention Isaac earlier as looking back, I know he was my first "heart dog" and for that, I need a chapter to explain.

If you Google "Heart Dog" many different things come up but essentially, people claim that your "heart dog" is in fact your canine soul mate. Your "heart dog" is a dog that comes into your life and you connect in a way that you can't explain. You can't go shopping for a "Heart Dog" and just buy one, and sometimes you don't even realize they're your "Heart Dog" until you lose them. You know each other in ways that you can't explain and you have a profound deep attachment, a love, if you will, that you won't find with other dogs you may have had. That's not to say you didn't love other dogs but it's different and when you find that one, you just know.

I don't want any misunderstandings here. A dog is not a human being and a dog can't take the place of a human companion. I don't believe a dog will ever be able to take the place of a human. But if you're lucky enough, you'll find one that does become your "Heart Dog". And if you're truly blessed as I have been, you may even find another in your lifetime.

This is the part where I blather on a bit, maybe with a sense of arrogance even. I delve into this because I know

I have found my human soul mate with Tim and he is so important to me that he needs to be recognized here.

I grew up believing he existed and I prayed countless times that I'd find him, marry him, have children with him and get old with him. It took me a long time, longer than most, and I even gave up but I did finally find my soul mate at what I realize now, was just the most perfect time.

I'm not going to say that humans need each other to be whole, and I don't think your soul mate makes you whole. But your human soul mate knows you, they know even the stuff they don't realize they know. They don't make you better people but they help you and support you in a way that helps you grow to become that better person. Your human soul mate sees your imperfections and even though they may be annoying, really annoying, they can see past them to what makes you special. Your soul mate doesn't see your special qualities all the time because humans are not perfect. You are not perfect and neither is your soul mate, but they see your special qualities when it matters most, not when it's easy.

The important part about soul mates is that they don't come into your life at a specific time, or at a designated age, they come into your life when it's simply just the time it's supposed to be.

It's very similar to your Heart Dog, I don't believe you can go to the "Soul Mate" store and just get one. You can't wake up in the morning and say "today I'm ready, today I will find my soul mate". He or she comes into your life when it's exactly the right time and it's on you to recognize that.

For those who have been blessed enough to have had a human soul mate and a canine soul mate, you understand. They are completely different and yet so much the same. No matter what, you cannot and will not ever replace them.

I was blessed to have an amazing dog come into my life. His name was Isaac and he was a beautiful pure bred German Shepherd with direct blood lines on both sides of his family from Germany. He had a full coat, but not a long coat, with a mix of silver in his saddle and the patch between his shoulder blades. He was so incredibly smart and strong both physically and also mentally.

In Isaac's puppy years, he was a brilliant study. He pooped once on the floor and due to his own mortification at the stench, opted in true form and his elegance to never poop in the house again. Of course, throughout the years he had maybe three or four "booboos" but I'm not proud or ashamed to admit, as a human, I have as well, so who can judge?

I worked with Isaac and together we learned obedience, tracking, Schutzhund and of course through this time of learning, we bonded. While we learned together, I also learned so much by myself, of myself and of others.

I was slower than most to learn how to drive, maybe in part that was from genetics as my Grampa never drove and my mother never drove until a mishap with my sister caused an emergency visit. But to this day, my mother would rather not drive. I, in turn, never saw the point of driving as I had two legs for walking, a bicycle for longer journeys and a phone to call a cab or the public transit system.

Isaac was also my walking partner. I can only imagine the miles that Isaac and I put on together over our almost fifteen years that we had each other. During our walks, I talked to him and he listened to each and every word I said, unless of course, he caught scent of a child, then I was on my own while he tracked that child. But the minute he was done, he was mine again and he listened!

Further to that, Isaac was my ears and thus, my protection. He protected me and gave me comfort while we lived in some of the most violent neighborhoods in Winnipeg and I'm forever in his debt for that because without him I truly don't know if I would have survived that time.

I got really sick when I was just over twenty and ran a very significant fever for a number of days. During that time is when I also lost a lot of my hearing. I remember thinking when I got Isaac, I needed ears and he definitely became those for me.

Isaac learned commands in English, German, Spanish and even a little Japanese! What dog knows all that? I would tell you some of the commands but I just know I would butcher the spellings in the different languages. But he did know those languages and I don't know what else to say other then it was really cool!

One of my fondest memories of Isaac was watching him with his teddy bears. He never tore up his teddy bears, he'd just simply remove the plastic eyes and then carry them everywhere with him.

While watching television together, he'd start doing his classic head bobs on the couch as he was starting to fall asleep with one of his teddy bears in his mouth. If you looked closely, you would even notice him in his snoozie state sucking on them. It was during these endearing times that it was all I could do in my power not to grab him up and snuggle the heck out of him!

Isaac was beside me when my Gramma passed from Cancer and he let me grab on to him, bury my face in his fur and cry like I never thought possible. I had family to help me through this loss and I feel bad for not including them here but even with family, I was alone but not totally alone because of Isaac.

When you suffer loss of a loved one, there are times when the grief sneaks up on you and if you're "alone" you fall apart and no human is around to pick up the pieces. It was like that with Isaac and losing my Gramma. There were times where I could be doing something, so minimally like washing the dishes and just out of the blue, my knees would weaken and there would be this hole in my heart. The tears would stream down my face and I'd gasp for air, Isaac would be there and together he'd help me wait it out until it passed.

Over time, my hearing got progressively worse to the point where I needed hearing aids but simply couldn't afford them and so, I became even more dependent on my Isaac. This was okay though because again, I had Isaac, and he stepped up for me. He stuck to me like glue almost knowing I read off him what was going on in the outside world. Watching television, I could tell the difference between a car pulling up to the neighbors, a bird chirping, or the mail man at our door just by the way he looked and how he carried his ears.

I mentioned Schutzhund training earlier. Isaac and I did this because his intelligence and constant wanting to work, which is typical for Shepherds, gave us no other option I felt. I'm not going to go into a long discussion about Schutzhund but it's a very challenging sport for dogs and their owners covering obedience, tracking and protection work. The "Protection Work" isn't to say you turn your dog into some kind of scary, vicious beast like so many seem to think. In fact it's quite the opposite; you're teaching them discipline and self-control and most importantly confidence in themselves.

Let's face facts, all dogs whether they're poodles or German Shepherds, they come with the basic instinct of fight or flight when put under stress. If a poodle bites you, you will feel pain, possibly even require stiches but chances are, you'll survive pretty much un-scathed. With a German Shepherd or any other large breed dog, a simple bite can prove very dangerous and even life changing.

Schutzhund did not teach Isaac how to attack and bite. But it did teach him that he could and should only do so under my control and say so. It also taught him that before he ever should escalate to biting, his bark should be worked first. It taught him self-confidence and that his bark really meant something and typically that he only needed to bark.

Don't believe me? Out of the almost fifteen years I had my Isaac he never bit once but he did save my life from an intruder with his hold and bark. He literally kept the bad guy pinned against the inside of my front door until the police came to pick him up. After medical examination of the bad guy, he had zero breaks in his skin and openly admitted the dog "paralyzed him" with fear.

Throughout his life, Isaac proved to be the best tempered dog I'd ever known.

Here's the part of the book where I introduce Isaac's dog. I don't know how to explain it other than that! I had a dog named Isaac and he had a dog named Vegas. This is to say that I accepted all responsibilities for Isaac and all his training. On the other hand, I negotiated with Isaac that if he opted to keep Vegas, it would be Isaac's responsibility to train him, take him outside for potty time, nurture him and love him.

Isaac and I lived on Furby Street at this time in Winnipeg. Furby Street was located in south, downtown Winnipeg in the heart of what I called "Nasty-ville". I hear that at one time it was a nice neighborhood and if you could see past the constant police cars, garbage, dirty needles and occasional chalk outlines, you could see what potential the neighborhood had.

I wasn't scared of living on Furby because again, I had Isaac and it was truly amazing how he kept people "honest". Other than one drive by shooting that left a 9mm round lodged in the brick under my bedroom window, we were fine during our time there.

Isaac and I lived in a three story house which was divided into three apartments, one per each floor and ours was the main floor. Each floor had its own exit through the front door hallway as well as our own fire exits at the rear.

Again I remind you of my hearing issues and Furby was a particularly bad place for my hearing as the danger was near at all times and Isaac had to learn to differentiate between these threatening sounds.

A cop car with the siren for example he deemed not a threat. He'd look out the window but quickly return to my side when the cop car passed by. We had a local that lived close, although I never found out where exactly, that howled like a wolf as she pushed her empty cart up and down the sidewalk for hours a day. Isaac again, deemed her not a threat.

Quite commonly when I had to go grocery shopping, I would walk to the grocery store which was a mile or so away but with the heavy load of groceries, I'd call for a cab to take me home. On multiple occasions, the cab drivers would help unload my groceries into my back porch.

On one grocery shopping occasion, when I came back from getting a load from the cab, I noticed that the cab driver was not on my back porch. I guess I'd forgotten to lock my inside door and he'd taken it upon himself to enter my apartment. The funny thing is, as many good cab drivers as I have had experience with, this guy in particular creeped me out. When he had offered to help with my groceries, I had turned him down.

When I opened the back door, he was in my kitchen and asked me where my bedroom was. At this point I became terrified as I knew my gut instinct was right. I pointed to the shut door leading to the bedroom and as he opened it, Isaac came flying out at him!

Isaac put on the scariest display I'd ever seen and he chased that cab driver out of my apartment! I quickly called the police but because no crime had technically happened they stated they had no recourse and all I could do was lodge a complaint with the cab company, which I did.

Here's the classic story line coming and get ready for it!

It was a dark and stormy night. Most everyone in the neighborhood was snuggled up in their apartments, littered with silver fish, mice, and an occasional cockroach, including myself. But Isaac was acting weird. He wasn't agitated per say, but pacing, whining and definitely unsettled. I'd seen him show "alert" and this wasn't it but again, he was obviously unsettled.

As the rain came down, thunder crackled and lightening lit up the sky, Isaac became more and more agitated. He was never nervous during storms and so finally, I decided maybe I'd missed the potty cue and decided to try taking him outside.

I got his leash, put on my shoes and the more we readied, the more excited he got. As I started to head for the back door which was our usual potty routine, Isaac started to panic and pulled me to the front door.

The minute I opened the front door, he bolted like a rocket out into the front yard, ripping the leash right out of my arm and ran towards the bush.

Instead of peeing, he sat down, starred at me and started whining even more intently. As I approached the bush, I noticed a small ball of, well I'm not even sure what. What I learned quickly under investigation was, it was a puppy. A puppy that I'd learn later had been set on fire, was covered in mud, terribly dehydrated and shaking terribly.

Isaac and I rushed him into the apartment and I immediately called a cab so as I could take this little fellow to the vet.

The vet confirmed that this poor little pup had burns and was in deplorable condition. His condition was beyond dire and to the point where he might not live. It was solely on me to decide whether or not to continue medical treatment.

I opted at this point to give the little fellow a shot at life even though the vet bills could prove to be costly. I was a receptionist at an accounting office at the time, and only lived in that neighborhood because I had limited funds and could only find a place there that was cheap and would allow Isaac.

The next day, the vet called to update me and stated that the little guy was doing well. In fact, he was really doing well and if I wanted, I could even take him home. That's when Isaac and I had the talk. I already had enough responsibility. If Isaac wanted this little fellow, it was completely on him to take the responsibility but I wasn't in the position where I wanted another dog.

Either way, I named the little guy "Vegas" as the vet kept saying words like "luck" and "beat the odds" so Vegas seemed like an appropriate name.

Again, Isaac stepped up and raised Vegas. He taught Vegas to go outside for the use of the "facilities", and taught him the basics like sit before supper time and even sit outside the bathroom door to wait for me in case I tried to sneak out the back way that wasn't there.

I say Vegas was Isaacs's dog and it was totally true. I could tell Vegas "sit" and he'd look at me like I had two heads, then he'd look at Isaac who would sit and then he'd copy Isaac. As long as Isaac was around, Vegas was a very obedient dog, any other time and Vegas was dumb as a sack of hair. That may not have sounded nice but sadly it was true. Having said that, Vegas grew into a pretty good dog albeit a bit wound up and again, not the brightest, but this could have been due to the trauma he suffered at such a young age.

For a visual, Vegas was a medium sized "shepherd, rat, kangaroo, and goat" cross. He had these long tufts of old man hair growing out of the inside of his ears. Let's just say, Vegas was not known for his good looks, but I still did love the little guy.

It took Vegas a solid year or so to "trust me" and allow me to snuggle him as I did Isaac. I can only imagine what that little guy went through, but I took my time with him and just let him come to me and deal with me on his terms. Given all the circumstances, he proved to be a very loving little guy although he remained hyper, and even seemed to border on neurotic. Vegas always had that amazing bond with Isaac. With Isaac, he was totally safe, as was I.

When I moved onto Furby Street with Isaac, the smartest thing I ever did was sign a lease for year long rent. I remember that night as the landlord was quite shocked at my request and didn't even have a lease available. In this neighborhood, typically all people were month to month renters.

The second night on Furby, he brought me the lease and I signed on to rent for a full year. That night after signing, was the drive by shooting that scared the crap out of me and made me second guess my decision!

Everything happens for a reason. I have always said this and always will and signing the lease was another case of this exact thing.

After Isaac, Vegas and I had lived on Furby for about six months, one day walking home from work, I noticed a high volume of people with their belongings in shopping carts walking down my street.

As I approached my house/apartment, I noticed an eviction notice on my window. When I called the landlord, he stated it was effective immediately as a company had purchased the whole block with the intent of demolishing all the old houses and putting up a seniors' apartment.

I remember stating that I appreciated his circumstances but I had a lease, had always paid on time and never had any complaints lodged against me. As far as I could tell, the lease was a legal obligation for rent and I could contact my lawyer for conformation of my legal rights, but if he wanted me to leave it would be in his best interest to make me a deal.

My deal was, I had moved onto Furby to save money in order to buy a house. I had been saving my money for a down payment and had financially budgeted it to take me the full year to accumulate the funds. However, if the landlord was to make up the difference, pay for my moving expenses, allow me to take all fixtures including fridge, stove, washer and dryer from my apartment, then I would consider leaving.

He flatly turned me down but the next day I called the local newspaper and informed them of the circumstances and how evil this landlord was for tossing people out on the streets and how dangerous it would be to put seniors into that neighborhood. The news story broke the next day and following that, I got two very important phone calls.

The first phone call was from my mother who was mortified that because of Isaac and I being on the front page of the newspaper, all her co-workers and friends now knew I lived in one of the worst neighborhoods in Winnipeg. This was followed by her even further embarrassment that I was being evicted from it!

But the second phone call was from my landlord and in order to rush his deal through, he agreed to all my stipulations.

Striking while the iron was hot, I found a house that fit my budget and within two weeks of my eviction from the previous neighborhood, I became a proud first time home owner in the North End of Winnipeg! Isaac and Vegas now had their own yard with fencing all around and I no longer had to take them out on leashes for potty time!

At twelve, Isaac had a seizure and a stroke. It took me months, but I rehabbed him back to a fairly good condition. We still got to go on our long walks but in the winter he needed "grippy" boots so as he didn't slip and fall on ice. He was slower, but we still managed to keep our paces.

What was difficult during this time was him and I realizing he could no longer make his running mid-air catches of my Frisbee throws. I could tell it bothered him, and at times he even looked at me like he felt he was letting me down but we simply threw out the frisbees and never did that again.

At thirteen, I noticed a lump forming on his left back leg by his bum. The vet confirmed that he had an anal gland tumor aggressively forming. Surgery was not an option for us as simply, Isaac was old and every day was already precious and a blessing. The good news was that due to the stroke he'd previously had, the vet felt that he likely didn't feel any pain at that time. I don't think he ever did feel pain from this tumor, if he did, he certainly never showed it.

The prognosis was that this tumor was going to keep growing both inside and outside if I denied treatment. Given Isaac's age, it was both mine and the vet's decision to not do treatment and just let Isaac live out what time he had left. We weren't sure how slow or fast the tumor would grow but it would continue and either prevent him from pooping thus causing death or it would rupture and Isaac would bleed out.

Just before Isaacs fifteenth birthday, I let him outside like every other day when I returned home from work and watched through the window. I had started watching the dogs potty as the vet had recommended I insure that Isaac was monitored closely to see that he was "regular". We knew that if he should start having difficulties, the outcome was not good.

As I sat perched on the couch with my nose pressed to the window, I noticed Isaac was straining badly for the first time. Further to that I could see he was also bleeding badly.

I let him in with tears pouring down my cheeks, squeezed him so tight and called my Aunty Dee. As my voice choked, I asked Aunty Dee if she was able to take Isaac and I in for his last vet visit.

While I waited for Aunty Dee to arrive, I allowed Isaac to do what he wanted in the house. He played a few minutes with Vegas and then proceeded to snuggle me on the floor and I held him tight knowing this was going to be one of our last snuggles together.

Aunty Dee only lived a few minutes away from me but it was odd, time seemed to go so fast and yet so slow. I was eager to get Isaac to the vet because I worried he was in pain, yet I knew that the vet visit would result in me coming home alone. The rest is sort of a blur but she got there quickly and we were off to Isaacs last vet visit.

By the time we got there, Isaac was really weak from the loss of blood but he still mustered everything he had for me. We walked into that vet clinic with his head held so high and proud and me trying so hard to choke back the tears. At the front desk, I announced with a shaky voice that Karen and her Isaac were there. I had called ahead to the vet and they were pre-warned so they got us into an operatory quickly.

In the operatory, Aunty Dee, Isaac and I sat on the floor. I think Isaac knew, he didn't fight anything. He was just tired now and he placed his head in my lap. He looked at me as if he was almost sorry. I'm not sure what he would have to be sorry for, he was an amazing best friend! I made sure to whisper that in his ears constantly. I told him how I loved him, and how it was okay to leave me as I'd make it. I told him I'd never ever forget him and everything he did for me.

The vet came in and with Isaac's eyes still focused on me, the vet slipped the I.V. into his leg. I watched my beloved Isaacs eyes slowly close and him slip away from me.

I have such a hard time as I write because one chapter? My Isaac was so much more to me and all I've written about him is one chapter? I'm crying right now like I'm back on that floor with Isaac's head in my lap with his life slipping away in every drop of blood and all he gets is one chapter? One chapter in a book that maybe nobody will ever even read, written by a "numbers girl". I'm just a normal girl who can't spell worth a damn, and sure as hell doesn't know anything about grammar. I don't consider myself an author by any stretch and never ever did become a vet.

I had a person once ask me "why would you ever cry over a stupid dog?"

If you've ever let a dog truly know you, you know him or her, and let them become part of your "family", part of your life, then you understand.

I do believe they have spirit, and I do believe they have feelings and can love. And I do believe they go to heaven. And I like to believe, Isaac understands how much he meant to me and how much he did for me. This chapter is probably the most important chapter because after everything Isaac and I went through, the most valuable lessons he taught me, I'd use to fight for Gunner.

Karen gets chosen by her "little blue boy".
Photo credit : Aunty Eileen Bennett

3 ~ AND THEN CAME GUNNER

At Isaac's first stroke, it was painfully obvious to me that there would come a time where I was going to be alone. Alone living in a nasty area of town and without my ears and protection.

I'll openly admit, this time in my life was particularly difficult as while my aging Isaac sat beside me, I started researching his "replacement" and I felt like a "cheater". How weird is that, I mean this is a dog, only a stupid dog right? I felt like I was cheating on my best friend. I knew Isaac's time was running shorter and here I was, looking for a replacement? How could I ever replace him?

The truth of the matter is, I was terrified. I lived in a poor neighborhood that had drugs, gangs, gun shootings and death. I was losing my best friend but also my ears and my protection and facing that, scared the hell out of me. I started my research and Isaac helped me every step of the way.

The more I read on breeds, traits and behaviors the more I realized that I really liked the German Shepherd breed. But as I looked at German Shepherd breeders, the more I felt overwhelmed at the thought of the "replacement' dog always being compared to Isaac and probably always falling short.

So here I was, needing protection, intelligence, loyalty, fearlessness, strength and whatever breed I picked, it needed to be as far from looking like a German Shepherd as possible.

I had "raised" Isaac "successfully" from a puppy into a full grown German Shepherd who lived a very long, happy life. He was an amazing dog and no one could deny that! I literally felt at that time that I obviously knew everything I needed to know about raising a dog and in particular a working dog.

When I started looking for my next dog, I did my "due diligence" and read constantly about a variety of Working Dogs. I spent hours with Isaac talking about Rottweilers, Dobermans, Giant Schnauzers, Bouviers, Malanois, and even went back to St. Bernards. However I started to notice that I was starting to read more and more on the Doberman.

Doberman Pinschers are considered people-oriented dogs that are affectionate, even sweet with people when they are socialized and trained properly. You can read that on multiple sites online and it's true. I know many Doberman owners say that once they have a Doberman in their family, they'll never have any other kind of dog! They say they're special and in my heart and mind they truly are.

It has been documented that a rescue Doberman after a few short weeks in his new home, saved the family baby by grabbing the baby and throwing it out of harms way from a poisonous snake. In that story, the family was mortified that this Doberman would grab the child and throw it naturally assuming that it was in fact a vicious attack! When they noticed that the Doberman had been bitten by the toxic snake, they realized that what looked like an attack was actually the works of heroics. In that story, the Doberman almost died from the snake bite but did recover after intensive vetting.

Another story had a mamma Doberman go countless times into a burning building, each time coming out with one of her puppies only to leave it curb side and return back into the burning building. She only stopped when she had retrieved all of her puppies. Again, an act of heroism.

A woman with Alzheimer's survived seventeen hours lost in the woods, confused and alone. What kept her calm through the whole ordeal was the fact that her Doberman never left her side. The woman stated that she wasn't scared because her dog was with her the whole time until she was rescued. When she was found, her Doberman even tried to accompany her on the ambulance ride to the hospital.

Many are unaware, but during WWII, approximately 75% of dogs used during combat were Doberman Pinschers with the other 25% being German Shepherds.

The island of Guam which has been an American territory since 1898 had been held by the Japanese for two and a half years until the U.S. Marines landed to retake the island. The Marines took both the 2nd and 3rd War Dog Platoons to assist in this venture with the War Dogs "jobs" being to explore the island's cave system, detect land mines and protect sleeping soldiers.

Currently, a bronze statue stands of a Doberman named Kurt at the War Dog Memorial along with 24 other brave Dobermans whose names are also inscribed on the memorial.

Kurt has been attributed with saving the lives of 250 U.S. Marines July 23, 1944 on Guam. Brave Kurt went ahead of the troops, pointing to alert them to a presence of approaching Japanese soldiers. Sadly, Kurt was mortally wounded by a Japanese grenade and became the first to be buried in the National War Dog Cemetery located at the Naval Base Guam.

There are multiple stories of Doberman heroics and amazing pet Dobermans but most people only hear of the attacks or vicious Dobermans. I'm not sure why this is other than maybe as humans we have a tendency to focus on the negative a lot more than the positive. I have always prided myself on my ability to see the positive and from what I researched, there was a lot of positive on the Doberman.

Further to all these great stories, in my search for my new puppy, while I wanted a puppy with Isaac's traits, I also wanted a puppy that didn't remind me of Isaac as I worried I would compare the two. Isaac had a full coat, long body, and a tail that cleared the whole coffee table off when he wagged it. The Doberman breed on the other hand, was completely the opposite in appearance but yet shared very similar traits!

Breed standards for the Doberman said short coat, tight and square body, and a nubby for a tail that couldn't move a fly when wagged. And let's face facts, they looked scary! I didn't want temperament scary but I wanted others to see him and to think "holy crap! VERY scary! I'll go rob the next house!"

The Doberman breed, was said to be highly intelligent, agile, and powerful. They have a very strong working capability, and are very loyal to their family which in turn results in a protectiveness. I spent almost two years reading about Dobermans and learned everything I could with Isaac's support.

I learned that Dobermans aren't just scary black dogs with cropped ears like in the movies where they attack everyone with frothing mouths. They come in four "allowed by standard" colours: black, red, blue and Isabella (or fawn).

I read up on possible "health issues" including Cardio Myopathy, Thyroid problems, Von Willebrands Disease and Wobblers. I read that while I spent a half hour each day brushing Isaac while watching Jeopardy on the television, this new puppy might only need a wipe down with a wash cloth for grooming. I read that a Dobermans life span sadly was not that long, many saying that nine years was a blessing. The more I read on the Doberman the more obvious it became, and after weighing all the pros and cons, Isaac and I decided that my next breed would be a Doberman.

As time went by, Isaac's tumor grew and started applying pressure on his anal gland and a discharge of stinky fluid started to secrete. While I shaved the area so as I could have access for cleaning to prevent open sores, I decided that I needed to start researching for Doberman breeders. With Isaac missing all his hair on his one hind leg, we took the next step together and went back to the computer.

I know many are sitting here now wondering why I didn't get a rescue, why didn't I "save a life", why wasn't a cross breed good enough. Was I too arrogant and I NEEDED a pure bred?

Not at all! I mentioned before, I've had crosses, and I've had rescues but when you commit to a dog you have to insure you are getting what fits your family.

I had very specific needs, and I felt at this time a purebred Doberman would suit those needs. I will also state, that at this time in my life, I also had Taxi, that crazy little rescued terrier cross and loved her dearly. But as great a killer she would prove to be in the future, she wasn't much of a deterrent when it came to a hopped up on drugs gang banger with a gun. A Doberman looked like he "meant business"!

So why research breeders?

There are piles of "breeders" out there, some good and some bad just like any other group of people. But if you take time to research your breeders, you will find them all different, and sometimes significantly.

Isaac's breeders were the ones who got Isaac and I involved in training. They knew Isaacs father most but also his mother and all their traits, medical history and so forth.

Lawrence and Karen knew from their "lines" that their puppies proved to be workers and they wanted owners that would work with their puppies to insure that their needs were met both medically, and mentally. Throughout the years with Isaac, if I ever need any help or had questions, Lawrence and Karen were a phone call away and only a fifteen minute drive.

When I found Gunner's breeder, I was looking for a "different" kind of breeder. This time I knew everything. I would never need help or support, just a quality puppy. Because again, I knew everything! How quickly I learned that though I knew "stuff", I sure as hell didn't know everything.

The next few years would prove to be the most humbling time and biggest learning experience of my life.

Coming home from Isaac's last vet visit, I remember my Aunty Dee talking and crying and it was all like a really bad dream. I'm quite certain that she was saying very kind, loving and comforting words but I sincerely don't remember a word she spoke. When the car stopped, I left the bloodied sheet in the back seat and walked alone into the house to "hair bunnies" floating on the floor that belonged to my Isaac. I'm not sure if I even said "goodbye" to Aunty Dee.

I'll openly admit, when I opened the door, both Taxi and Vegas welcomed me home but I didn't even see them. In fact, I think I even resented them.

That night I was so alone, so scared, and just so empty that I didn't sleep a wink. I heard things that weren't there, I felt Isaac move when he wasn't there, I could even feel the bed moving with the breaths he no longer took.

I was very lucky as my employers were amazing during this time and more supportive than most. They had told me that when the time came that they would accept nothing other than me taking time off and as much as I needed. Further to that, they also said that when I was ready, they would support my new puppy endeavors by helping anyway possible up to and including my new little puppy coming to work if I wanted.

That first week without Isaac, I didn't sleep, didn't shower, barely ate and sure as heck didn't go to work. But then, one morning I woke up, woke up in the sense that I felt something other than pain and started living again. I cried the whole day but I cleaned every square inch of that house and it was a big house.

I cried as I vacuumed up Isaac's "hair bunnies". I cried as I packed up Isaac's dog dishes, leashes and toys. I would love this new puppy, but there was no way in the world he'd touch Isaac's stuff! And I literally broke down when I came across his winter ice grippy booties. That's when I went back to the computer and sent out three emails to my list of chosen Doberman breeders to see if they had litters.

I feel ashamed of writing this because I'm still shocked that Isaac was gone only one week and there I was emailing breeders! But here's the thing, when you lay in bed at night, in a neighborhood where you know that it's so far from quiet and yet all you hear is silence, that silence is truly deafening. Isaac was my best friend but he was also my ears.

Turns out that the day after I put down Isaac, Gunner's litter was born to a breeder that lived a few hours away. I think that maybe that was another one of those "it's meant to be" times.

My email to the breeder came when Gunner was six days old and although she said it was still early, she felt confident that she would have eight puppies for me to choose from, four blacks, two reds, one blue and one Isabella. She called it her "rainbow litter" as although she knew from the genetics of the mother and the father that it was possible, it was not expected to get all four allowed colours in a litter.

I booked our first visit at the litters' five week mark. I knew that they wouldn't be ready to go home yet and knew this would give me more time to complete my research and I guess, just simply prepare myself and of course puppy proof my home.

I still didn't drive at this time but Aunty Dee quickly and eagerly volunteered a number of her friends, commonly referred to as my "adopted aunts" for the road trip out to see the litter.

On that day, Eileen, Shirley, Pat, Aunty Dee and I all piled into Eileen's van and we started the three hour journey out to meet the breeder and her litter.

It was a terrible day for driving! We were in the dead of winter and true to Winnipeg weather, the wind was blowing the snow strongly which made for the sight of "snow snakes" slithering across the highway. As I stared out the window, my aunts chattered away. This was another time when I don't remember much of what was said but I remember "you don't have to pick one if you're not ready".

I think I was the one saying that, repeating it over and over in my head.

A few hours later we arrived at the breeders.

It was a nice house. Not ritzy schmitzy as most people would believe but it was a nice house. Very clean, and we were immediately invited into the kitchen with eight little Doberman puppies. I don't say or write this with much enthusiasm because truthfully, I wasn't enthused. Don't get me wrong, puppies are amazing but everything and everyone were just too damn happy for me.

We were offered a place at the kitchen table but by the time I had taken a chair, all my aunts had tossed their jackets into a corner and were sitting on the floor with puppies all over them. Again, too much happiness.

Reluctantly, I sat down on the floor too, but only because they did, I would have preferred I think to just sit at the table as none of these cute little puppies were Isaac.

I watched and watched as puppies climbed and barked, played and peed now and then and then went back to playing. But there was one little guy, the "blue boy" just sitting across the kitchen doing the same damn thing as me, watching. He didn't play, he had this look on his face like "look at these idiots".

I'm not sure how long we were there but the puppies started to tire and slowly but surely, they started curling up for naps. Some of them curled up to each other, and others climbed on my aunts to snuggle in. That's when that little blue boy looked at me, crossed the floor and climbed into my arms. I reluctantly held him up and he looked me straight in my eyes and I pulled him right into my chest.

He had the most beautiful eyes I'd ever seen in a puppy, they were almost a lavender colour with little brown speckles! And his skin was so funny, it was like he had too much, almost like a Shar Pei with all those rolls and I remember telling him while he was in my arms to pull up his pants because he had all these little rolls of skin by his butt.

As I held him, he didn't make a peep just a long puppy sigh and he just nuzzled his nose into the nape of my neck. It seemed like only seconds passed and he was far off to sleep and with the wonderful puppy smell and velvet like fur in my arms, it happened right in that moment. I found my new friend!

My aunts and I left the breeders to "think about it" but there was no thought in my mind. He was going to be mine!

We went into the small town and found a restaurant where we proceeded to have lunch. The topic at lunch table was of course that cutie-pa-too-tee blue Doberman we had just seen. I could still feel him in my arms sleeping!

As we sat there, I reminisced about Isaac when he was a little puppy and it was hard. So hard.

I could remember the first time Isaac was "attacked" by an empty plastic Coke bottle I had dropped by accident and he so strongly rose to the occasion and did his first little aggressive bark! I remembered him being so mortified at all the monsters on the street when we took our first walk together on garbage day but with puppy hackles up, he braved each of them. And I remembered Isaac always chasing his tail, how on earth was this guy going to do that when all he had was a teeny tiny nub of a tail?

We paid our lunch bill, went to the bank where I withdrew my deposit and headed back to the breeders. I gave her the money, and while she wrote up a receipt, I gave my new little boy one last hug. And then came Gunner!

Gunner's first car ride home with Mom, Dad and I.

4 ~ OUR FIRST CAR RIDE

Leaving the breeders with only a little piece of lined paper that had a hand written note of "deposit accepted on blue boy" was so difficult.

As much hurt as I was still feeling in loosing Isaac, now for some reason, by leaving that little blue boy on that kitchen floor, that hole in my heart seemed even bigger.

As we yet again braved the winter roads on our way home, off and on, I cried. They were tears of joy, of sadness, of loss, loneliness and even fear. I felt so terribly overwhelmed with all these feelings but didn't question my decision for a second. Somehow, deep inside, I honestly felt that Isaac would really like this little guy and this I really held onto.

My aunts couldn't stop talking and laughing about all these cute little puppies they'd just snuggled and played with! How that little black puppy tried shaking the toy all big boy like. How the little red girl was beating up on her brother and seemed like a little trouble maker in disguise. My aunty Shirley had become particularly fond of the little Isabella or fawn girl that had fallen asleep in her arms.

After the longest few hours of my life, Eileen pulled the van up in front of the house I had bought in the "North End" of Winnipeg. With a pile of hugs and congratulations I left my aunts and headed into the house alone.

The North End of Winnipeg wasn't nearly as bad as Furby Street but it was still dicey. I no longer saw the shooters anymore but could still sometimes hear the odd gun shot. People rarely robbed us in this neighborhood because where I was in particular was a poor neighborhood and well, my neighbors were the robbers. I hate to draw this analogy but my "robbing" neighbors were just like dogs, they didn't like to "poop in their beds". They went to the "nice" neighborhoods to score loot and typically brought it "home" for the sale.

As I walked into the house, again Taxi and Vegas greeted me at the door and for the first time, I noticed that poor little Vegas wasn't himself. He'd taken the loss of Isaac so badly, and he was so lost without him. I prayed that little Vegas would take to this new puppy and maybe "step up" like Isaac had for him. However, we wouldn't know if that was to occur for the next few weeks, until that little blue boy was ready to come home.

Those three weeks again dragged on like months.

I kept in constant contact with the breeder by sending emails every second or third day. I consistently asked in the emails how "my little blue boy" was doing. I realized after that even though I'd only spent two hours with him, I guess because of Isaac's loss, I felt that I was going to lose him too and more loss was just too much for me.

I remember thinking, if the breeder decides to sell him out from underneath me, I have enough emails to prove he was supposed to be mine. There's no way a court of law could ever dispute that the little blue boy wasn't mine. How crazy is that? I'd never sued anyone but still in grief, I wasn't mentally clear, I had fear, a gripping fear of more loss. All these irrational thoughts consumed me and my days as I waited for the time to come when I could bring him home.

I think also that I didn't really believe that I could love another dog again because of Isaac. Pardon me for saying this but I think I expected this to be more of a business transaction only where I was securing my protection. But in those few minutes where that little boy had been so snuggled into my neck, I had in fact fallen for him and hard!

Finally the three weeks passed and this time, again because I couldn't drive, mom and dad agreed to take me the three hour drive to the breeders to pick my little blue boy up and bring him home.

It was an early March Saturday morning that we set out on "Operation Puppy Pick Up". The sun was brilliant in the vibrant blue sky which caused little sparkles to shine in the crusted snow that had started to melt. It was indeed a perfect day that for most I'm sure would give life to hopes and dreams.

As we drove again down the highways with miles of prairies on each side of us, I slipped again into all those deep consuming irrational fears. They hit me in my core and hit me hard taking my breath away. As mom and dad made small talk I lost my visions of hopes and dreams and replaced them with what the feeling I knew best at that time. Loss.

I had talked over the phone with the breeder the night before in preparation of picking my little guy up but all the "what ifs" started popping into my head. What if they moved? What if I got there and the little blue puppy was gone? What if the breeder had changed her mind? The fear and nervousness was gripping!

Mom was excited for me but dad, not so much. He had misconceptions about the Doberman breed and was literally concerned for my safety. The number of times he mentioned to me that "those dogs attack their owners for no reason", well, I'd be rich if I had a nickel for every time he brought it up.

Mom on the other hand just kept replying, "Oh John, Kari will be just fine, you said the same thing about Isaac and he was a wonderful dog!"

We finally arrived at the breeders right on time and to my absolute shock, my blue boy was there! I was actually going to get to take him home!

This visit was completely different then the first visit with my aunts. Today, when I walked into the kitchen, only my little blue was there. All the other puppies were in the back room with their mom. I'm quite sure they could be heard making their puppy sounds but I completely voided them out. With all the relief in my heart and the terrible weight lifted finally from my shoulders, I truly could only focus on my precious new friend! In fact, for the first few moments I saw the breeders' lips moving as she talked to me but I heard nothing coming out of her mouth. I was here for my little blue boy only and finally taking him home!

The puppy's tails had been docked at about three to five days after they were born which we'd seen at our first visit. But their ears had only been cropped twelve or so days ago, they were still somewhat fresh wounds. I had read about this but wasn't quite prepared.

As my little blue boy walked around the kitchen I noticed quickly that his ears were standing straight up and wrapped in bandages! I have to admit, as I was seeing this for the very first time, my heart hurt for him but he didn't even seem to notice.

Over the next hour or so, the breeder moved into teaching mode and I was her student. She explained that for the next few months and possibly even up to six to eight months I would have to continuously take out these little tapes, clean the area and then repost his ears. She also stated that I could do this two ways, I could be rough about it and forceful causing it to be a terrible experience for both the puppy and I. Or I could be caring, gentle and take my time in this and make it a part of our "grooming routine".

She also explained that for many different breeds of dogs such as Great Danes, Schnauzers, Boxers and even the Brussels Griffon for example, the time can be significantly different but that it depends on the length of the crop.

I had done a lot of research on the cropping of ears and docking of tails and it seemed to be quite controversial. Some people outright swore it was cruel and in-humane where others stated it was done on each breed for a particular historical reason.

I don't expect anyone to change their position on whether they think it's cruel or not, in fact many of you reading this might be judging me right now for "supporting this" but what I can tell you is this.

I loved this little puppy and had always put the dogs in my life first and before mine which sounds crazy but it is true. I have heard constantly from people that breeders are out there only to make money and piles of it. So take into consideration, if I'm a greedy breeder only in it for the money, why on earth would I spend more money, which comes out of my "profit" to professionally have their ears cropped unless it was for what I truly believed in? Why would I as a "greedy breeder" crop eight puppies which I would have to continuously clean daily until they left for their homes unless again, I believed there was a valid reason?

When researching the reason for cropping the ears of various breeds, many legitimate reasons came up depending on the breed. But for the Doberman it said that back when Louis Dobermann developed the breed, he did so with the intent of the breed protecting him during tax collection. It is said that long floppy ears are an easy target for attackers to grab or for other animals to bite. Historically, the crops were made a lot shorter and removed a lot more of the ear to suit this purpose. Over time for the most part, crops have been made longer for appearances. Many people will say, "well you're not collecting taxes now and you don't need to do this anymore." But then I have to say, after reading all that I did, I wanted my Doberman to have cropped ears.

Please understand, while I wasn't collecting taxes or wanting to be in a position of aggression, I was living in a neighborhood prone to violence and wanted protection. I originally picked the Doberman because it did in fact look scary and part of that "scary" was the ears.

When Doberman puppies are born, they have floppy ears and if you've seen a grown Doberman who was not cropped, they do somewhat look like Labradors. I'm not saying Labradors can't protect or be scary, but my hopes were always that the trouble people would see this obvious Doberman and walk the other way.

Again, many have in their minds their thoughts or position on cropping and docking, and all I can say in closing is that where I respect yours, please also respect mine. To the breeders out there that choose to have their litter of puppies cropped by professionally trained vets, I respect your decision. For people who take it upon themselves to cut puppies up with no training, knowledge or medical background, you shouldn't have any animals.

And please know this, because many provinces or states have now banned cropping, there is a significantly higher volume of irresponsible backyard breeders doing this practice themselves on kitchen tables. They have no training or knowledge and are too lazy and cheap to pack up their litter of puppies and travel a long distance to a vet where this procedure is still allowed.

Anyway, back to my blue boy! The breeder placed a blanket on the kitchen table, placed my little boy on it and began to show me how to carefully remove his tapes. To my surprise, he just sat there starring at her with a goofy puppy look as she showed me how to take out the "tapes". Together, the breeder and I cleaned and washed the area at the back of the ears where the stiches had been and now little scabs remained.

She then proceeded to bath him in her kitchen sink which took minutes as opposed to the length of time it took to bathe Isaac. As she towel dried this little guy I remember that the next stage for me usually was a twenty minute blow dry brush. However, this little guy seemed to be dry just from the towel!

There were still little scabs on the backs of his ears but for the most part, they were all healed up. After this, while my blue boy played on the floor and chewed on my ankle occasionally, the breeder taught me how to take popsicle sticks, paper towel and Jonas medical tape to re-wrap new "posts" that would be placed in the "bell" of my new Doberman puppy's ears.

At this point, she taught me how to carefully re-apply the posts and how to tape the ears around the posts. This was something I needed to learn and learn well as I would have to repeat it every few days for the next few months.

Soon, my little un-named blue boy, mom and dad and I were ready to go and then again, the loss of Isaac was felt. But this time I also had a bit of excitement in my heart. I think it was puppy breath!

For anyone who has smelled it, oh my, it's the most incredible smell ever! It's better than fresh cut grass, better then popcorn, homemade apple pie or cinnamon buns and is definitely better then new car smell. The only thing that measures up to puppy breath smell is maybe, maybe, fresh cleaned baby butt with that powder smell. And I still think that puppy breath smell is a smidge ahead of that but that might be because I haven't had my own human baby but I have had puppies.

While we drove the three hours home, my little blue boy snuggled in my arms and slept while I breathed in that amazing puppy breath. He was a great car rider and slept the whole way!

We stopped at the half way mark gas station where I lovingly woke him, put his brand new leash on and took him out of the car and placed him on the ground. With a big, tired yawn, he squatted and peed like a little rock star. Call me crazy, but I was proud, damn proud of my new little boy! How smart was he already!

Back in the car, my little blue boy again snuggled into my arms and went right back to sleep without any "boo hoo hooey" or cries. While we drove, mom, dad and I talked about the "little blue boy".

He wasn't blue so much as a gun metal colour, like a silver grey almost, it was simply gorgeous. And his eyes, he still had those beautiful lavender with brown speckled eyes. That's when I decided, my little blue boy was now my "Gunner" and it was perfect for him!

Not a peep came out of Gunner that whole way home and it absolutely amazed all of us. He didn't squirm, try to climb around, he just slept and snuggled the whole way in my arms.

Again, Taxi and Vegas greeted us at the door upon our arrival home. This time they both noticed that a weird smell was coming from my arms and they wanted to meet him!

Gunner on the other hand just looked down from my arms with no real concern or interest. He seemed to feel totally safe and secure. Carefully, I obliged and placed little Gunner on the floor and the meet and greet went well. Taxi had more of a "m'eh" attitude to Gunner but Vegas did seem impressed and immediately started trying to teach him how to play with the tennis ball.

I was quite sure that this day, was now a fresh start for me. It was going to be different now as for the first time in weeks, I was more excited now than I was lonely, fearful and empty. It was a new day that promised a future of fun!

I was right about Vegas as Gunner really put a spring into his step. Taxi didn't really bother with Gunner that much as he was a tad rough with her but Vegas quickly adored Gunner and started teaching him the ropes.

Going outside the front door meant negotiating four or five steps down from the landing into the yard. For the first while, Vegas would slowly take each step looking over his shoulder as if to prompt Gunner as he took over exaggerated hops with his little body. When they both reached the ground Vegas would almost seem to congratulate him with a fun bark and with Gunner in tow, the two would head off to the nearest and only tree.

By that tree, again Vegas would watch to insure that he had Gunner's full puppy attention and it was only when he was sure he had it that Vegas would proudly lift his leg and pee on that spindly tree. After Vegas was done, Gunner would sniff and then to Vegas' disappointment, squat and pee.

Vegas who was usually so rangy and uncontrollable became very patient and kind as he dealt with Gunner during his puppy stage. Gunner was absolutely amazed at their tails and consistently tried to play tug of war with Vegas' in particular. In his patience, Vegas would pretend to not notice this new dead weight hanging off him and would just simply drag Gunner around.

I was quite shocked at what Vegas put up with as Gunner was always climbing on him and grabbing him with his needle sharp teeth but Vegas seemed to love it. I guess for him, he had quite a fluffy coat so maybe the puppy needle teeth weren't that bad but I couldn't imagine it myself and cringed while I watched!

For Taxi, she wouldn't put up with Gunner's ill puppy behaviors and after a few quick snaps at Gunner, he learned very quickly that she wasn't nearly as receptive to his rough play as Vegas was. Gunner learned REAL fast not to grab Taxi or her tail ever. This had resulted in him trying one of his tug of war games that ended quickly with her doing her most aggressive snarl, and a quick cheek grab. When she let go, Gunner came a running with Vegas in tow straight into my arms crying.

From this point on, as much as Gunner wanted to play with Taxi, Vegas always seemed to put himself in between the two of them to insure no one got hurt or offended.

By the five month old range, Gunner was the same size as Vegas but it bothered Vegas not. Vegas seemed to realize Gunner was just a baby and needed to learn things from his knowledgeable direction.

Together the two of them smelled flowers from the outside barrier of my garden. They chased bugs and occasionally ate them but most importantly, Vegas did manage to teach Gunner to eventually lift his leg to pee. The rite of passage for all male dogs was reached and it was a prideful moment for Vegas! A true sense of accomplishment.

Taxi, Vegas and Gunner each had their own kennels upstairs in my bedroom but I very rarely locked them in. For the first while during the puppy pee training phase, Gunner was the only one at night to be locked in his kennel while the other two either slept at the foot of my bed or in other various locations.

Taxi, however, soon learned if she wanted quiet time from this rough housing little monster, she could go inside hers and with her claws, shut her own door. Gunner never did figure out how to open it.

I think the cutest thing for me was how Gunner slept and how he woke up.

When the pack decided to have nap time, they commonly would all jump onto the couch for a little snooze. But for Gunner, instead of sprawling out like Taxi and Vegas, he curled up real tight in a ball and always reminded me of a little deer.

Vegas was usually the first to wake up and he'd immediately start barking to awaken Gunner to go outside but Gunner was always so slow to wake up. In fact, when Vegas would start this, I'd get off the love seat and crawl across the floor on my hands and knees slowly to where Gunner was on the couch and with his little groggy eyes looking at me, I'd nuzzle my face into him quietly saying "Wake up, wake up my little Gunner-roo!"

Upon this, Gunner would smoosh his face into me and almost like a cat start rubbing me. While he did this, he'd let out these little tiny yawns oozing puppy breath. He would do little puppy stretches and after a few minutes of this slow wake up snuggle, with the "squintiest" of eyes smiling, he'd eventually wriggle out from underneath me. Slowly and very dramatically, Gunner would then slide off the couch.

It was only after we did this whole wake up routine that Gunner would be ready to yet again take on the new world and under Vegas' direction learn how to be a grown up Doberman.

Above : Puppy Gunner
Below : Gunner snoozing at work in his kennel.

5~ SIR FARTS-A-LOT

This chapter is not about that amazing puppy breath smell that brings immediate warmth to your heart. This chapter is about puppy breath's evil twin brother called "wall paper peeling, make you wretch, burn all your nose hairs, toxic flatulence". It won't be a pretty chapter but it is an important part of the story.

On that lovely early spring day, during the long three hour ride home with mom and dad, we were often "visited" with a stench so violent that it often made us dry heave.

Now that I had my freshly bathed new little puppy safe in my arms, I appreciated the sun shining so brightly in the sky as we again drove through miles of prairies. I now did have new hopes and dreams and had so much excitement in my heart for what the future would bring. I had visions of puppy goofiness, trouble making episodes and my days being filled with puppy breath snuggles.

These visions would be violently torn down with one whiff of the air and completely destroyed while my stomach rolled with such an extreme nausea that I worried I would vomit all over my beautiful little puppy.

I tried desperately to figure out what this stench was and I truly couldn't place it.

At first, I remembered the time that in the dead of summer when I was a youngster, a rotting beaver corpse had washed onto shore by our dock. I remembered how repulsive it was until finally someone in the family had "geared up" and removed it. Before that body was taken to the dump, no one could walk within thirty feet of that thing it smelled so bad.

This smell was much worse than that and we couldn't get away from it! It wasn't skunk, we weren't passing any sewage lagoons or water treatment plants, those were all pleasant smells compared to this.

Of course for the first few "assaults" nothing was said in the car because I assumed mom and dad were doing the same thing I was. Trying to figure out what the hell it was, where it was coming from and what could possible explain this. But, just like the prairies, it kept coming on mile after long mile.

I finally accepted the fact that someone had to be passing gas but who and had they seen a doctor about this?

Mile after terrible long mile, the air would clear for a few moments until again we were hit upside the head with the stench. There was no happy chit chatting happening here as there was on the ride out to the breeders. Instead, there was dead silence and I can only assume that mom and dad were thinking the same as me, it was someone else and it would have been impolite to make mention of it as vile as it was.

Minutes dragged on into the first hour, and repeatedly the silent aggressive stench would envelope us and someone would give out a cough, slightly scratch their nose or ever so casually look out the window in what seemed to be almost a silent prayer. I think on one attack, dad actually whimpered like a little girl.

Truth be told, I openly admit that I was silently blaming mom. Mom, if you're reading this, I'm terribly sorry for that but you know as well as I do that dad would rather spontaneously physically blow up then pass gas "in public". If dad had gas and had to pass it, he'd pull over, make some crazy excuse for needing to get out of the truck like testing the density of the snow or something. But, I could see you trying to sneak off a few as any normal person would.

Either way, as polite people are, we pretended, as tears ran down our cheeks from time to time, that the stench wasn't there. Little Gunner slept right through it all, didn't move a muscle and even seemed to have a teeny weeny smile on his face.

After the pee break at the halfway mark where Gunner pulled off his first Rock star status, we set back out onto the highway again without a word being said. With that little love bug back asleep in my arms, the stench turned our lives upside down yet again and continued to do so regularly throughout our long trip.

Finally and to my complete surprise, mom yelled out in panic "For the love of God, who's doing that" which quickly resulted in Dad exclaiming he thought it was her. As they both looked at me to pass blame I quickly denied it as well!

After a lot of laughter, while rolling down all the windows in the car, we realized it was little, tiny, cute, puppy breath and stinky butt, Gunner. But come on now, who could blame him? He was in a bouncy car, first time with strangers, away from his litter mates, we all just chalked it up to stress.

Never in a million years would I ever have expected that such a tiny, precious little creature could produce something so toxic! It was true though, that stench was coming from little Gunner as he laid there in my arms with that little smile on his face.

Gunner came home on a Saturday, and Monday was his first day of work! I had mentioned how supportive my employers had been with the death of Isaac and with welcoming arms, they asked that Gunner come to work with me.

Over the years I had graduated from a basic receptionist at the accounting firm, to assistant with case files. After logging a lot of hours there at the accounting firm, I had been offered and took the role of Bookkeeper at a dental office. After a few years of Bookkeeper, the dentists promoted me to Financial Controller which assisted me in landing a Financial Controller position at a small Marketing Company.

After a few years at the Marketing Company, I had been pursued by two gentlemen to take the Financial Controller position at a company they had recently purchased but wanted to be "silent" in. At this company which sold environmental cleanup products and safety gear, I had my own office that I shared with the owners of the company but they'd rarely be there. Due to the fact that they were rarely there, they only had an office chair and foot stool each which allowed room for a kennel and toys for Gunner behind my desk.

I think he howled off and on for the first week but as the books had recommended, we started a schedule of routine which consisted of regular activities that Gunner quickly adapted to and in no time he was working well as the new mascot. Except for the farting of course.

Every morning Gunner and I arrived by cab and while I went to my desk to start my day, he went to his kennel where he could snooze or play with toys. We usually had a morning fifteen minute coffee and potty break and then returned back to our work station. At lunch time, he and I joined the other employees in the lunch room where, while we ate, he stayed on his bed with his lunch and chew toy, but when everyone was finished, he got to play. We then again returned to our workstations until afternoon coffee and potty break. The end of the day brought us to our cab ride home.

Monday thru to Friday we followed this pattern and in no time Gunner was potty trained as well as learning basic puppy obedience and socialization which I read was a requirement for Dobermans. But no books prepared any of us for the farting.

Our home life consisted of arriving home and playing with Taxi and Vegas but mostly Vegas until Gunner's "yawnzie monster" hit. Together, we'd all curl up on the couch for a quick cat nap where usually Taxi and Vegas were at my feet and little Gunner curled up on my chest. I did this specifically because I knew I wouldn't hear his whines to go outside but I would definitely feel him stirring on me and it worked perfect!

As days went by with such a tight schedule, Gunner, Taxi, Vegas and I all settled in quickly but Gunner's gas persisted.

The beauty of having a "breeder" is that again, you have someone to call to ask questions. I did so and at this time, the breeder and I chalked it up to "settling in".

As weeks went by, we maintained our work and life schedule and sort of tried to get used to the gas issue.

Gunner was fed before work, a little snack at lunch time, and again when we got home. I insured that he didn't get human food or in between snacks and watched him constantly to make sure he didn't eat weird things in the yard such as the occasional bug with Vegas but his gas persisted. Again, when I say gas, that's an understatement.

It was the most horrid stench ever that was even worse than rotting beaver corpse, skunks and sewage plants combined!

After multiple discussions with the breeder and also numerous vet visits, I changed dog foods and we followed the schedule again and waited. A few months would pass, we'd go back to the vets' and the recommendation would be to change his food again. Sadly, nothing seemed to work and Gunner quite lovingly got the nick name around the office of "Sir Farts-a-lot". Simply, everyone adored him but he sure stank up the place!

This always ate away at me. Not for the obvious stinky situation that his hideous butt flare ups were but I knew that when I got gas, particularly stinky gas, it usually meant I had a belly ache to go with it.

Gunner didn't show signs of abdominal pain, and as stated, I did take him to the vet regularly about this but he did have soft poop. In fact, he never really had a "normal poop" for a canine. He was incredibly regular with pooping but it was vile and thank God he learned to only do it outside quickly.

For experienced dog people, "normal poop" means you can pick it up with a baggie pretty quick after it happens. With Gunner, you always wanted to wait a day or so to give it time to dry out and firm up otherwise it would be quite a mess. Sadly, even after waiting days before picking it up, it would still prove to make a mess that needed a quick hosing down.

I will openly admit and also reported to the vets, that he did seem to have "cow patty poop" or diarrhea a lot. But he'd be examined, tests were done on his stool, bloodwork taken on him, the answer always seemed to be to try a different food and so I followed directions.

It wasn't until Gunner was almost two or so that although he still had gas regularly, at least it seemed to be somewhat under control. But to be honest, to this day, I can't remember him ever having a "rock star" poop that you could pick up right away. And there were still multiple times that he completely cleared a room with his gas.

As much as Gunner was loved at work, and as noble and intelligent as he was, he never did shake the nick name "Sir Farts-a-lot".

Just to insure that you truly get the picture, I've picked up vomit, cleaned up diarrhea, and dealt with some pretty "bad" situations when it came to animals and humans for that matter but only Gunner to this day has ever been able to make me heave.

I think the worst thing was, you never heard it coming. One minute everything is right in the world with visions of unicorns dancing softly in the clouds and pretty sparkles of all colours floating magically around, and the next minute you were violently consumed with complete horror and briefly lost the will to live. That was Gunner's farting and it was constant.

I don't know how a "real" author would write it but, the house smelled like rotting ass, the office smelled like rotting ass and there wasn't enough Febreeze or deodorizer in the world to take it out. But we all loved little Gunner and so we put up with it! Besides, it wasn't like I wasn't trying to resolve the issue, I was working on it with the vet.

They say "paybacks a bitch" and I tell this next story running the risk of self-humiliation.

Work progressed and Gunner grew at work, learning more and more obedience and socialization. Add to that, I consistently introduced him to "fears" so he could, with my assistance, overcome them and build his self-confidence.

He got to climb on boxes, sit on moving fork lifts and be pulled around on skids with pallet jacks in the warehouse. This was all part of me trying to grow him to a well-adjusted, confident working dog and he loved every minute of it! The farting seemed to be just part of the package and I made sure no one lit a match around us.

In November of 2008 I would personally take the leap and I decided that after all the cab fares to and from work, it was time to get a car and my drivers' license. Work was only about a five minute drive away so I figured I could handle the short drives.

Because my mom and dad had one they so enjoyed, I followed in their footsteps and I purchased my first car ever. A brand new, sparkly, Kiwi Green Ford Escape and the pack and I were free! By July of 2009, I had decided that it was time to leave the North End of Winnipeg and move out to the country and loved every minute of it including the 35 minute drive to and from work.

I handled the drives well as did Gunner. By that time, he was about a year and a half old and had learned to lay in the back with his paws and chest on the centre arm rest so he could "assist" with the driving.

It was so cute because I'd be driving and he'd be staring straight out of the front windshield watching the roads right along with me. Gunner quickly learned that the stick at the left side of the big round thing made me look over my shoulder and then the car would change lanes. Every time I touched that stick, Gunner learned to shoulder check with me.

If we got close to other cars that weren't moving in front of us, he'd quickly look to the floor because there was a box there that he learned that if I stepped on it, the truck would slow down. Sometimes more quickly than others!

And the stick on the right side of the big round thing was really neat because it made two more sticks outside on the window go back and forth and sometimes even water came out! Driving was a hoot with Gunner as he was so intrigued with all that went on!

But not so much with "Sir-farts-a-lot".

We would be driving down the highway on a beautiful day whether it was spring, summer, fall or winter, again we would, in this beauty, have unicorns dancing in the clouds with the pretty sparkles until he'd let one "rip".

Thank God I learned how to not panic but it would leave me dabbing my eyes and trying to stay focused on the road. But I loved him and he loved me.

Truth be told, I think he got a kick out of it. In fact, many thought he had started farting on purpose as he seemed to almost laugh at us as we gagged.

Here's the story that is my humiliation and my victory at the same time.

I don't know what I had eaten but I had the most terrible upset stomach ever. I had managed to make it through the work day but purposely stayed late as I was unsure if I'd make the drive home on country roads with no bathroom in sight. When I finally felt like I had a thirty minute window, Gunner and I bolted to the truck and headed home.

Somewhere at about the fifteen minute mark into our drive I started feeling pain and my stomach started the well-known by many, "gurgle of death".

I remember Gunner actually hearing that gurgle of death as he even cocked his head to the side as it happened. But we persevered and drove on.

As the gurgling continued and intensified I was left with the inevitable decision of how to manage the situation. There's no way to sugar coat it, but I had to fart. I won't lie, I feared farting in this condition. But I also feared not farting. So with the slightest of leg lifts, no one but Gunner in the truck with me and the radio blasting, I let out the smallest of farts.

Gunner didn't hear anything, but when the waft of air rose, I looked dead into eyes thru the rear view mirror and for the first time ever, my blue boy turned green as tears started to form! It was beautiful!

He jumped up and in between sneezes he actually heaved multiple times. Through the rear view mirror, I watched him stagger to the back door and claw the window wildly begging for his escape even though we were travelling at over a hundred kilometers an hour. It was like he didn't care that his life would be lost if he left the vehicle at that speed. He was willing to take the gamble just to get away from the smell!

For me, it was beautiful and I refused to roll the windows down.

To this day, the Escape back window doesn't properly defrost as he cut some of the wires with his nails while he madly clawed at it that day, but it matters not because it was my victory and yes "pay back" is sometimes a bitch!

Above : Gunner being the "perfect office working" dog.
Below : Gunner in the lunch room at work, thinking
INSIDE the box as opposed to OUTSIDE the box.

6 ~ YOU'RE PUSHING MY BUTTONS

In true to form working dog personality and puppy inquisitiveness, Gunner loved to learn new things and figure things out. I worked with Gunner in this and supporting him in his snoopy endeavors. If Gunner found things that were "scary", I came to his side and made him work it out until the scary stuff passed and he "figured" it out. In my mind, this helped him develop his self-esteem which I felt was so important.

It sounds silly talking about dogs and their self-esteem levels but it was something that proved crucial to me while I trained Isaac in his protection work.

I learned that dogs that typically bite people actually did lack in self-esteem a lot of the times. Particularly dogs that ran around you to bite you from behind as they couldn't even "face you".

Isaac, who oozed self-esteem never bit anyone and truthfully, he didn't seem to fear anything and therefore never really reacted out of that fear. This was my intent with Gunner as I never wanted him to react quickly in the moment as that could result in a quick bite.

As a puppy it started on our first cab ride to work. He loved sitting on my lap, looking out the window as cars passed by and he always had such an inquisitive look on his face while he did so. He'd press his teeny tiny nose up against the window so tight he'd make little steamy circles and snot bubbles, just because he wanted to get a little closer to the outside world flying past.

On that cab ride while Gunner sat so perfect in my lap, I rolled down the window by using the button. Gunner was absolutely mortified and that little barrier with the steam circles and snot bubbles immediately became that glass monster and it could move by itself!

Seeing the fear, I held him closer and expressed excitement in the glass monster. And together, we learned how it didn't move on its' own but we could control it and all by the simple push of a button.

I know it sounds crazy but the minute that Gunner learned with my assistance that by using his toe to push the button made the glass move was literally a "light bulb" moment for him. From that minute forward, he was a button pressing fool.

It's funny how we think we teach good things and then years later realize what a stupid thing it was to do.

With Isaac, the worse thing I ever taught him was to scratch at the door when he had to go out to go potty. At first glance, that seems like an awesome idea. But as the years went by, not only could I not hear Isaac scratching at the door due to my hearing loss but I also never had an outside door again that wasn't all gouged up like a cougar lived there.

The second bad "trick" I taught Isaac was how to play fetch exclusively by catching the Frisbee out of mid-air. Again at first thought, this was amazing and to watch him was incredible as he got crazy air time in these leaping catches. It was a beautiful sight to see until he had his stroke and he could no longer do it. Then it was heartbreaking seeing him want to and not be able to. Further to that, the impact on him hitting the ground left a lot of times where I worried about his hips or twisting something as he got older.

With Gunner, I vowed to only teach him "good tricks" so as they wouldn't come back to haunt me as the door scratching had. But as much as you think about various things, you can never really see the full ramifications until they rear their ugly heads. This was the case with Gunner and his window button pushing which would extend past windows to pretty much any buttons you can imagine!.

I was late to change over from a land line to a cell phone because simply, due to my significant but not total hearing loss, I could still somewhat hear using the "old school phones".

Gunner loved attention and his nose would get quite out of joint if he didn't get the attention he wanted and when he wanted it.

It seemed to me that Gunner "allowed" me to be on the phone in conversation for about ten minutes. At the ten minute mark, he would find his loud obnoxious squeaky Cuz and chew on it wildly beside me while I tried to chat. I would tell him to "knock it off" which of course he wouldn't.

After about five more minutes of the squeaking while I was on the phone, I'd finally take the cuz away from him and put it somewhere high up. I laugh as I type this because when I did that, the look on Gunner's face was always so priceless! He would truly look shocked at my behavior and it was obvious he found it unacceptable!

Gunner, in his frustrated retaliation for the Cuz now being out of reach, and me STILL on the phone would be to march right over to me and, using his nose, push the button on the phone that disconnected the conversation. But the funniest thing was he would then march away in anger, lay down and stare at the wall as he no longer wanted attention from me! He was mad!

I rarely watched television as I was now on an acreage and had a lot of yard work. But when the weather was the pits, the pack and I would retreat to the house and settle in for a good movie in the dvd player.

This was a great snuggle time until Gunner decided he was done snuggling and wanted to play. Then he'd march over to the dvd player and push the button with his nose, popping out the dvd and ending the movie. I'd march over, put the movie back in, Gunner would march back and pop the movie out. Back and forth we'd go like an old fighting married couple until of one us finally gave up and went sulking away in our defeat.

One of my favorite relaxing down time activities was doing Sudoku puzzles. I had multiple Sudoku books and pencils laying around the house in strategic spots that I could settle down and grab one. I still have those books and if you flip through the pages, you'll find many puzzles with what looks like child scribbles on them. This is because Gunner would reach that magic ten minute mark and felt I'd spent more than enough time on the puzzle and would shove the pencil while I tried to write. Just like the movie watching, I would continue to do my puzzle and he would continue to shove the pencil. Thus, all the scribbling and even in some cases, torn pages.

Manitoba winters can be quite harsh and as Manitobans we've learned that plugging in our vehicles is a requirement on many a night to insure they start the next morning. As the winter gets harsher, the day light also decreases until finally we're driving to work in the dark and getting home in the dark.

When I purchased the Ford Escape, I had done so simply because mom and dad had one they loved. It had proven very reliable and handled well the dropping temperatures of our winters.

Sadly, my Escape seemed to be quite the opposite. At least three times a week, I'd have to call dad to come over and boost my truck as it wouldn't start in the morning even though it had been plugged in. Many a time, I was late for work and the frustration led me to the Ford dealership on a number of occasions having a hissy fit at the front counter about the "crappy piece of junk" I'd bought from them.

At the Ford dealership, they ran tests, changed wires, checked the block heater and swore up and down on numerous occasions there was nothing wrong with the Escape. They even changed my battery a number of times as they never seemed to hold charge.

The problem was answered when coming home from work one day with Gunner.

I turned off the truck and watched in the mirror as he pushed the centre roof light button and it turned on. He did it so matter of fact and perfectly timed that I knew this was habit but truthfully, I'd never noticed him do it before!

Here I'd thought that when I turned the truck off, that light automatically came on and it does do that if you manually set it to. But I hadn't manually set it, yet every night we'd leave the truck and the light would be on. We'd head into the house and I'd never look back. The next morning of course, the truck wouldn't start.

This time however, when I got into the house, I did look back and that centre light stayed on for more than an hour until I bundled up again, went outside and pushed the button to turn it off and called dad immediately. I certainly don't claim to know anything about cars so when I told dad what I'd witnessed and my theory, he started laughing. It was his opinion that by Gunner turning the interior light on and it remaining on all night, it was killing the battery in the truck.

Where I appreciated that Gunner thought it was important for him to illuminate our way in the dark, I certainly didn't appreciate, nor did my bosses or co-workers, us arriving to work late on a regular basis because the truck wouldn't start.

Damn button pusher! I never did go back to Ford and apologize as I was too embarrassed to tell them that it wasn't a "crappy" Ford as I had stated so many times loudly, but a really smart Doberman.

I had to watch him like a hawk until finally I used duct tape to cover the light button and that did not impress Gunner at all. For weeks, he tried to push the button through the duct tape but the light didn't come on and he'd leave the truck in a huff. Eventually he did give up on this but I never did remove the duct tape until years later which of course left glue residue all over.

Gunner's "button pushing" continued and grew into simply pushing things over if he had a "comedic moment" or temper tantrum which was cute but also very frustrating at times.

Many a coffee he spilled on me as the second I took a sip, he'd nudge the bottom of the mug perfectly and even "ninja stealth like". Upon spilling hot coffee all over me, he would sit back and almost laugh at me while I usually sat there using profanities and cleaned it up.

Gunner quickly learned how to kill the power to my computer hard drive and did so a number of times which even resulted in the "blue screen of death". At the vets' office, they learned to place objects in front of the hard drives in the operatory during our visits. I should say, they learned the hard way as even though I warned them ahead of time of Gunner's new trick, I guess they didn't believe me. We were led into the operatory, Gunner surveyed the area, walked straight to the hard drive which was on a stand Doberman nose level and with a steady nose push the screen went dark. No more appointments that day!

At the environmental company, Gunner used his ten minute pushing rule here as well. For the most part, he slept during the day but when he did wake up, he gave that ten minutes until he decided it was time for me to pay attention to him. He was now of good size and he would approach me as I sat working on the computer and he would start to push things on my desk.

He typically started with my computer mouse which was on my right side. If that didn't get attention, he'd tip over my stapler, my coffee cup or start pushing the papers around. I will say, I wouldn't "let him win" as this only fed him emotionally. As he would push things, I'd pretend to ignore him but I have to say that in my heart I laughed at his ingenuity. Eventually when it didn't work, he would get into his frustrated huff and go lay down in his kennel to chew a bone.

One morning, one of the owners came into the office and I can't remember exactly what the situation was but he was wound up. He stepped over the baby gate that kept Gunner in my office and went quickly to his chair. As was typical, Gunner got out of his kennel to greet him but this time the owner didn't even notice Gunner and was talking to me.

The owner had placed his papers and his coffee on his foot stool and didn't even pat Gunner as he stood there ever so patiently with his waggly nub of a tail! As much as Gunner tried, the owner still didn't notice him so he did what Gunner does. He got mad for being ignored and in his "fit of rage" he shoved the foot stool hard at the owner, banging his knees and knocking all his papers and coffee onto the floor. While the owner swore, Gunner seemed to almost stomp off to his kennel beside my desk and even shut his kennel door.

Gunner and Taxi had the occasional scraps as even though she was the size of a loaf of bread and he was a Doberman, she was the second in command under me in the house and she, in her mind, ruled over him and Vegas. And by rites, this was true, Gunner and Vegas did listen and respect her. Usually.

Taxi would take Gunner's bone on a regular occasion and Gunner would naturally get mad but wouldn't growl or snap. When the opportunity would present itself though, he would manage to pin Taxi between the couch and the coffee table. I would watch him watch her and he'd actually wait for her to go between the couch and coffee table and then he'd shove the coffee table as hard as he could. Then he'd manage to grab the bone and go lay down leaving her pinned. I would then get involved by rescuing Taxi and then taking the bone from Gunner and putting it up high.

Pushing buttons and shoving things was Gunner's "thing" and he got such a kick out of it but his favorite was always the automatic window button.

Oh the power he had if I took off the child locks! He seemed to understand this power as odd as that sounds. This window button was perfect, and particularly great if on summer days where we needed the air conditioning but yet Gunner wanted to bark at passing dogs. He could push the button thus unrolling the window, bark like hell at the dog, then pull the button to roll the window up again to keep the car cool. This worked fabulously in the winter time as well to keep the heat in yet let Gunner have his say. Absolute genius if you ask me.

I had mentioned that some of the physical appearance attributes that I liked about the Doberman was how they were so different from my Isaac, the German Shepherd.

The Doberman was short, tight body with short coat and a nub of a tail. One of the things that drove me crazy with Isaac was how he could clear my coffee table with one swipe of his wagging tail. I had quickly learned with Isaac that there was simply no point in having a coffee table as you couldn't leave anything on it. Because of this, I got rid of the coffee table.

With Gunner though, this would never be a problem and I was excited to have a coffee table again! For the first while, it was great being able to put stuff on the coffee table! Then Gunner learned to push things with his nose or shove things with his paws. Where his tail didn't clear it off like Isaacs', his attitude would, and when he wanted attention and didn't get it, he'd tip over drinks on purpose, or push books or magazines onto the floor in frustration.

In my stubbornness, I kept that damn coffee table but sadly, never had anything on it again because I knew nothing was safe with Gunner around!

Recently Tim and I decided to sell my Escape and it broke my heart. As I cleaned the Escape up, I cried when I saw that my Escape still had the scratches by the window button and glue residue by the roof lamp button because of Gunner. And of course the back window still did not defrost properly. I loved that Escape, it was a great vehicle, and never left me standing except for in the winter those few times but that was Gunner's fault not the truck.

At first I couldn't figure out why I was so upset about selling the truck and I think Tim had problems understanding it also. But I realized, Gunner and I did so much together and a lot of it was because of that truck and a lot of it was in that truck. That Escape wasn't just mine but it was Gunners also. Letting go was difficult because I felt like I was letting go of so many precious memories with Gunner.

At the end of the day, Gunner simply loved to push buttons and shove things. Many times he did it because he thought it was funny and he was very much the comedian. But he also learned that from me because it was so hard to hide the laughter on some occasions. As I look back, it was also funny seeing him do this because he got mad when he didn't get his way. There was a lot of character in that.

Either way, throughout his life, many a button he did push! Looking back, I so wish he was here today to push buttons.

Above : Gunner at his very first Conformation dog show!
Below : Thank you to Judge Judith Shurb on Gunner's
Conformation Group Forth!

7 ~ MY SHOW BOATING ROCKSTAR

The day that my aunts and I had visited the breeder for the first time, she had asked that I consider the possibility of showing Gunner. The breeder was very eager to show that little blue boy in "conformation" depending on how he turned out.

She didn't just breed two Dobermans together to make puppies and sell them, she was trying to get as close to breed standards as possible with her litters. She bred the Doberman to try to preserve and even further the Doberman breed as she truly did love the breed. This is why "good breeders" breed dogs, never for the money but to preserve and further the breed.

Great breeders actually accomplish that. Many of them, while breeding, submit DNA samples to try and understand and eventually cure a multitude of diseases that just don't affect some breeds but canines in general. For "good" and "great" breeders, they truly not only love their breed of choice but also all canines.

You can find a good breeder by asking if they test their dogs for a variety of diseases. Find out if they've x-rayed their dogs for hip and elbow issues if that's a common problem with their breed. Find out if they've done holter monitor testing for heart problems. Find out if they spent the money on these tests. Find out if they've invested money in showing their dogs and not just the dogs they're breeding, but the puppies that have gone to "pet homes".

A good breeder doesn't make a lot of money on a litter of pups after they've done all this. But they've spent the money to insure they're doing their utmost to further their breed. I can't remember ever seeing a "good breeder" show up in a fancy expensive car to a dog show, they're more inclined to have older vans or suv's. But they typically have signs on their vehicles that say "dogs on board" or so forth. They love their dogs.

In Canada, we have the Canadian Kennel Club or CKC as it's known. In the United States of America, their recognized body is the American Kennel Club or AKC. The two function very much the same. Having said that, the two do have differences in regards to some of their breed standards, breeds recognized as well as group structures.

Both countries offer a variety of "shows" that in combination can "prove" a very well-bred dog that follows its breed standards. You can enter in Lure coursing, Field Trials, Tracking and Herding, Agility, Rally Obedience, Conformation and more.

When I talk of a "standard", both the CKC and AKC have a standard that specifically describes each and every recognized breed in many areas from origin, general appearance, size, coat and colour, temperament and so forth.

As an example, the CKC breed standards for the Doberman state that the appearance is that of a dog of good middle size, with a body that is square: the height measured vertically from the ground to the highest point of the withers equalling the length, measured horizontally from the fore chest to the rear projection of the upper thigh. The Doberman should be elegant in appearance, with proud carriage, reflecting great nobility, and should be compactly built, muscular and powerful for great endurance and speed.

The point of having "standards" is because each breed has a multitude of purposes that they are bred for and their overall physical appearance in conjunction with their character traits complete this purpose.

The Doberman was originally bred by Louis Doberman in Germany in 1890. He was a tax collector as well as the local dog pound operator. He aimed to "create" a fearless, intelligent, agile dog to protect him as he did his collections and so overtime, came the Doberman breed.

If we look at the original Doberman and compare it to today's Dobermans, there have of course been changes but they are still somewhat the same with temperament being the major change in my eyes. The Doberman of today is, yes, still protective but the temperament has changed to make it more family oriented.

I had stayed in touch with the breeder because again, Gunner was having all the gas issues.

As Gunner grew, I watched to see if he seemed to fall within the breed standards for Dobermans which in fact he did. This was not because I wanted to breed per se, but because if the breeder had a high number of her puppies prove to be close to breed standards, then it showed that she was in fact working to preserve and further the breed.

After discussions with the breeder, we decided to enter Gunner in his first dog show for "Conformation" or physical appearance.

I'll openly admit, I didn't train him to "stand for examination" where the judge looks at his teeth and goes over his body. And I didn't do much leash work but he was so darned smart and we did do basic obedience in the warehouse, I figured he'd just ace it! What a fool I was!!!

I was so proud to see my little Gunner at six months of age go into his first dog show with a professional handler. He looked so darned handsome! Of course with him being a blue Doberman, he also stuck out like a sore thumb as the typical Dobermans were your black and reds. Everything seemed okay until the handler started to run him around the ring with the other Dobermans in his category to show off his "gait".

The other Dobermans ran on all four legs calmly beside their handlers where-as Gunner hopped on two legs like a kangaroo with his tongue hanging out of the side of his mouth!

Needless to say, that day the "points" went to one of the Dobermans that ran on all four legs. Personally, I felt Gunner should have got the points as he was definitely the most entertaining out of the bunch and he sure seemed to have fun!

As the months went by, I took Gunner to more and more Conformation dog shows and he quickly learned to stop the kangaroo bouncing that he did so well. Slowly, he started to earn "points" for wins as is required in order to gain his championship. The funny thing was, Gunner learned that when he got that little ribbon, it was a win and a very good thing! Further to that, when Gunner did get a win, I of course reacted so proudly and loving to Gunner that it reinforced this whole win situation. This all seemed to go straight to Gunner's head if you can believe it!

The shows were typically three day events and the pattern for Gunner was always the same. The Friday he'd forget everything he knew and would act like a fool and we'd go home ribbon free.

The Saturday is when Gunner seemed to pull up his socks and usually did quite well. Sundays is when he shone and typically got his wins.

Sundays were our "great days" at the shows, but they typically turned out to be our "crappy days" at the house as Gunner's attitude would get out of control. After returning from the shows on Sundays he got into the habit of lifting his leg in our house. He'd only do it once but he'd do it as if to say to myself and the pack that he was Mr. Fancy Pants Show Dog who can do whatever the heck he wants!

Where I adored him winning points, obviously, I did not appreciate him lifting his leg on the wall, the door, the stove, television, even Vegas or anything else in the house so I'd chastise him with a loud "bad dog shame!". He'd get all "woe begotten" and go into his kennel and his victory party was quickly ended. I always look back at that time and still laugh as he never peed in the house except for when he had a win in the Conformation ring. Even though I always chastised him, he always lifted his leg once on those Sundays. It's not like I didn't watch, I'd follow him around saying "Don't you even dare think about it!" Sure enough, just when I thought the moment had passed, he'd lift his leg.

I continued to show Gunner in Conformation with the help of professional handler and he "finished" his Canadian Championship at around eighteen months at a dog show in Brandon, Manitoba, which I thought was pretty darn good.

After he finished, and because he enjoyed it so much, I started to show him myself and together in the ring of the CKC, we both gained confidence and did in fact take a number of "Best in Breed" ribbons and even a Group 4th placement under the wonderful judging of Ms. Judith Shurb, which I will never forget.

Over time though, Gunner seemed to start losing interest in Conformation and because of that he showed his in-attention in acting like an ass at times. When I say he acted like an ass, I mean that he truly didn't seem to give a rip to anything I said in the ring and he just outright wouldn't listen.

Truthfully, I started to lose interest as well to some degree but him embarrassing me on a number of occasions helped in my decision to look to other CKC shows to work in and quickly we decided Rally was a perfect fit for us!

Rally Obedience is a wonderful sport for those that want to have fun in the ring with their dog.

I commonly refer to regular Obedience as more of a "military style" of obedience, you learn strict commands and patterns. In obedience you state a command once and the dog needs to do it.

Rally on the other hand has a number of "signs" that you have to follow as the judge sets up for his or her course. The judge "maps out" a course of these signs on pylons, each of those signs that have a command on them. Each course is different and Gunner never lost interest in Rally as it contained so much variety. He simply never knew what he was going to have to do.

Further to that, you could really talk to your dog and give him or her praise, clapping even at their successes and patting them. Gunner loved praise for doing "good" so he thrived on this as did I.

In order to prepare Gunner and I for Rally, we trained in our backyard or in the house. I say this as, if you're looking for something to do with your dog, please try this as I've watched so many people with all types of dogs have fun at this! It doesn't require perfection per se, it requires fun and bonding which I think most pet owners want to achieve with their dogs.

Rally did have a multitude of commands but if you broke them all down, they revolved around your basic skills. Gunner and I worked constantly to achieve solid sits, downs, comes, stays and of course heel. I then started to print out the various Rally signs and actually got little pylons that I could mount them to.

It's important that I say this here; Gunner and I never attended Rally classes, we learned on our own. This isn't to say you shouldn't try classes but I didn't see it as an option for Gunner and I because he was showing dog aggression. I wanted to be able to train relaxed and not worried that some dog would come up to him or that Gunner would get fixated on another dog and not train.

I've met many dog people who are looking to do something with their dog since then and I've always recommended Rally to them. Many times, I saw these people in the Rally ring after and they were having fun.

There was a woman I met at a dog walk function in Birds Hill Park while I was there for other reasons that will be mentioned later. As we talked, I found out that she had bought her husband a Beagle but sadly after a few years, her husband had passed suddenly. She was at the dog walk for her first time out alone with the Beagle but without her husband.

As we talked, she expressed that she was looking for things to do to bond with this Beagle the way her husband had. I quickly took the opportunity to suggest Rally to her as an option and even gave her names of Rally instructors that I knew. Quite frankly, I never thought I'd see her again, but I had hoped I had given her some help.

I was so very excited to see her months later ring side with her number on her arm as she got ready to go into her first Rally dog show! She was so nervous and I just said to her not to forget the purpose of Rally. Have fun! She did, and she and her Beagle passed that day with flying colours. To see the beaming smile on her face was absolutely amazing to me.

Over the years, I saw her numerous times in the Rally ring not only with her husband's Beagle, but she also got another Beagle that she participated in Rally with. I often wonder what ever became of her.

From what I understand now, CKC and possibly even the AKC now also allow cross breed dogs in the Rally venues so again, if you're looking for something fun, give Rally a try!

In Rally, there were different levels that you could graduate from once you achieved three passing marks. "Novice" had the dog on a leash. The next level, "Advanced", was off leash and had more commands added. "Excellent" was the final level, again, off leash and additional commands.

Gunner and I showed in Rally Novice for the rest of his show dog career due to the fact that he always had to remain on leash. Where Gunner had a lot of socialization, he had over time started to also show aggression toward other dogs. It was weird, he wasn't consistent with his aggression towards dogs. In fact some days he seemed to be friends with all dogs, other days, he seemed to downright look for scraps.

While talking to many different people about this, the feedback was always the same, he was an intact male (not neutered) and it could be that females in heat were around triggering this. For me, I didn't like the behavior at all and had never experienced it with Isaac but then again, Isaac had been neutered. Either way, I never trusted Gunner to be off leash as I didn't want to take the chance that he could hurt another dog.

Overtime in Rally, Gunner and I won multiple ribbons for a variety of placements but also numerous "high in Trials" as Gunner truly did love to do his Rally and it was a really good time for us! It was a time for fun, bonding and reaffirmation of our "commands" and always reminded him who was boss in our house.

For Gunner in particular, when he was "on", he had a complete blast and showed phenomenally. He literally would bounce like that kangaroo around the ring and this was allowed because we were supposed to be visibly having fun. As far as Gunner was concerned, everyone was there to watch him and only him and he was there to entertain his "public".

This led to a very unpredictable Gunner at times though. I truly never knew what I was going to get from him in the ring. Would he work "spot on" with me or was he truly there to put on a show for his public? And just what exactly would that show be?

At one show in particular, he was there for his public and not me at all. As we started our way around the course we came up to the sign that made him sit. I was to then move in front of him while he stayed and take one step back. I would then call "front" to make him come sit in front of me. This would then call on me to take two steps back and repeat and then three steps back and repeat.

Gunner, this time thought it would be great to catapult himself through the air at me like a rocket, jumping up, putting both paws on my shoulder, and give me a kiss that knocked my glasses off. That was not what the sign said to do. With Rally, you are allowed "two do-overs" where if you fail at a sign, you can retry it. So we tried that station again with the same results coming from Gunner and my now slobbery glasses landed on the floor again.

The more people laughed at the side of the ring, the more frustrated I got because Gunner thought he was being a comedian and "entertaining" which actually he was, but in turn we were failing miserably as a team.

Trying to take command of the situation, I firmly pointed my finger at Gunner and stated "stop!" He looked at me, looked at his public, looked at the judge and jumped up and bear stomped the Rally sign into the ground to show his disgust. We left the ring, him mad and me embarrassed.

Later in the day, the judge from that trial approached me and said that he'd never seen a dog give his handler the finger in the ring like Gunner had. We both laughed because it was the truth.

The next day, Gunner got a 99 out of a possible 100 in the ring. He still "entertained" and put on a show for his public, but he also worked as a team with me and I so enjoyed that!

I guess I write this chapter because some people think that when you have a "show dog" it's because you're arrogant or pompous. I wasn't as most "show dog people" aren't. I just wanted to do something with my dog that he and I enjoyed. I'm just a regular person like any of you.

Above : Puppy Gunner in his favorite blue fleece jacket.
Below : Older Gunner (around 5 years old) wrapped up in his quilt.

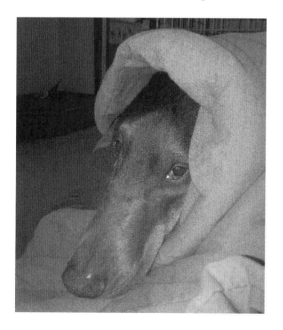

8 ~ SO COLD

From the minute I brought Gunner home, I recognized immediately that he always seemed so cold because he'd shiver violently. I could tell this wasn't a nervousness or a fear issue, he was literally shivering because he was so cold and when touching him, his tiny little body did feel cold. The shivering wasn't an ever so casual shiver that occurred now and then either, it was constant and reminded me of the many times I had inappropriately dressed for ice fishing days with my dad.

While I wasn't used to this sort of thing with any of the previous dogs or puppies I'd had, it made sense to me. Isaac for example was a full coat German shepherd, he had piles of hair for insulation and was a little teddy bear fuzz ball as a puppy whereas Gunner was pretty much "butt naked" with his thin short haired coat. Even Taxi, being a terrier cross had thin hair but still seemed to have ample hair compared to Gunner whom even had bare skin on his inner thighs and little belly.

I had picked up Gunner from the breeders home in March which was definitely not the coldest time for Manitoba weather. We were however still in late winter and early spring which meant our temperatures were still well below freezing. Add to that, Manitoba and Winnipeg in particular is well known as having terrible wind chill factors which led sometimes to weather warnings of exposed skin freezing in seconds.

Taking little Gunner outside to go potty proved to be quite a feat particularly in the morning before the sun was up as the minute I opened the door to the outside world it was obvious he'd rather be anywhere but outside! I couldn't blame him though because I too didn't want to go outside and I was bundled up for the extremes when I took him out. I couldn't even imagine heading out there in a t-shirt and shorts particularly when the wind was blasting arctic air!

I had to time it quickly so as I could get him to potty before he was too consumed with his shaking to forget about the purpose of the early morning adventure out in the cold temperatures. Quickly though I noticed that little guy even try to "hold it" which on occasion led to us coming in to warm up but yet not make it out again due to the little puddle he left at the door.

I'll admit, I didn't scold him for these booboos as again, I could completely understand and felt that things would get better over time.

In the long run though, I think this made his potty training easier because we played inside and only went outside quickly for potty reasons only. Hence he never pottied where he played and he also learned that the faster he went, the faster he'd get back in the house. But I will say, seeing this teeny tiny little guy outside shaking and crying was so terrible hard on me. There were times where I did consider trying to paper train him in the house instead as I felt so bad for him. We did though persevere and in no time he was potty trained. As difficult and heart-wrenching as it was, I recommend it as being the best time of year to potty train puppies.

I was never a fan of having any of my dogs allowed on the furniture, in fact, Taxi was the only one allowed up on the couch and bed because she was so little. Isaac was allowed on the bed eventually while I slept but that was due to my hearing issue getting worse as I wouldn't hear him if he barked while I was sleeping but I would feel him move or jump off the bed.

Little Gunner however, refused to lay on the floor because again, it was too cold for him. Some would say he was just being a little suck of a baby but I envisioned me laying on the bare floor in a t-shirt and shorts and couldn't imagine it being comfortable by any stretch.

Again, I adjusted for Gunner and when he was little and unable to jump onto the couch, I placed a foot stool for him to use. As Gunner got bigger he of course no longer required the footstool to get on the couch but I kept it as I noticed Taxi had started to use it.

Due to this "coldness", I also made accommodations and worked with Gunner by raising the temperature in the house from 68 degrees Fahrenheit to 72 degrees Fahrenheit which seemed to help a fair bit.

When Gunner was older and I had the Escape, I always pre-warmed the truck with the auto start when we went for car rides so as to insure his comfort. Gunner seemed to pick up on the truck being pre-warmed and this lead to the creation of what would become our favorite morning "blitz" game.

Just as we were ready to leave for work, I would stand at the door with Gunner in "sit", and with me looking at him and him looking at me, I'd say real slow, "On your mark.... Get set.... Annnnnnd.... Go!!!!" Upon the "go" Gunner and I would race to see who could get to the truck the fastest. It was funny though because the longer it would take me to finish the "On your mark, get set, go", the more false starts Gunner had and more quivering in anticipation he'd do.

Thinking back, I actually giggle a bit because once we'd get into the truck I'd look at Gunner and quite commonly his tongue would be hanging out the side of his mouth and he'd be panting heavily like he'd just done the fastest sprint known to mankind and miraculously averted the most incredible danger ever! He always did beat me though but had to wait of course for me to open the truck door.

I always insured warm thick blankets were around whether they were in the truck, at the office or in the house should he need to snuggle in for warmth and this he became a champ with! If he required them, he'd quickly start digging at them and in no time would be completely cocooned in them.

When Tim joined our life, he quite commonly referred to Gunner as the "Baba with his babooshka" as Gunner covered his whole body and head with his blankets only leaving his nose and sometimes eyes out.

I have a confession of sorts here and apologize in advance if I hurt anyone's feelings. I personally always thought clothes on dogs looked down right stupid and pitied the poor souls forced by their owners to wear such ridiculous outfits. Well except of course for Halloween as that was just plain cute. But for Gunner, it had a purpose, even a requirement so he quickly obtained a full wardrobe of fleece coats.

After buying multiple fleece jackets which never really seemed to fit properly or cover him enough, I even kicked it up a notch and purchased sewing patterns and started making my own for him. This left me the availability to modify them so as to cover more of his belly and even have an add on feature of a turtle neck which I could pull up high on him.

Depending on his/my mood, he could sport his blue fleece with plaid cuffs, his dapper maroon fleece, or a variety of solid colored fleece in of course "boy colours" that complimented his steel grey hair colour. On special occasions he could even kick it up a notch and go Doberman gangster style with my creation of his camouflage fleece and turtle neck ensemble.

At the end of the day, he was still a "tough" Doberman even while sporting clothes. As a little puppy, people seemed to admire the cute puppy with a jacket. As an adult, nobody made fun of him within ear shot of me because again, he was still a tough Doberman.

At work, Gunners' kennel had a blanket, plus he wore his coat and he had an extra quilt. Quite commonly, he would go into his kennel and before you knew it, only his nose could be seen as he'd managed to maneuver his blankets so he was completely covered.

Again, it all made sense to me given his short coat, so even in the dead of winter, where the temperatures reached to -38 degrees Celsius, temperatures around us were always made comfortable for me in a t-shirt and shorts which typically also meant it was comfortable for Gunner and his coat. As you can imagine, this resulted in high heating bills but I was more than okay with that.

Gunner was also a blue Doberman. If you read up on Dobermans, yes, they have a short coat but the "dilutions", or the blues and Isabella's, actually have less hair follicles per square inch then the black and red Dobermans. So again, this "coldness" made sense to me.

Looking back, there was typically only two or three months out of the year when Gunner didn't wear a coat and that was in the dead heat of summer. But even during this time, inside air conditioning sometimes proved to be too cold for him and the fleece coats came into play again.

In life, you can do your research, you can learn and if you do your due diligence you can expect that certain things will happen and so you prepare yourself for them. But also in life, sometimes you get a curve ball.

This "coldness" was a bit of a curveball, as was his nasty gas issue, but you work with them. And really, they weren't really big issues at all, there's a heck of a lot worse issues out there.

Although this coldness was difficult for me to work with, what I hadn't realized was the outside exercise limitations it would create.

Back with Isaac, it was nothing for us to go outside and play in the snow even as a puppy for sometimes and hour or more but with Gunner, he couldn't and wouldn't have any part of that. Even with his fleece on he'd potty and then race to the door. This lead to me trying to exercise Gunner mostly in the house or the warehouse. As a puppy, this wasn't so much of an issue as at home Vegas helped out a lot with the two of them wrestling. As an adult though, Gunner needed to run outside but couldn't a lot of the time.

The additional problem though came with Gunner wearing the fleece jackets a lot or so I thought. Even though I washed them often, he quite commonly got rashes and "pimples" in his arm pits, back, head and belly area. These pimples seemed to appear everywhere but particularly on his chin and the top of his head whereas the rashes appeared more in his arm pits and belly.

We had along with the gas issue, also seen the vet about the rash and pimple issues and it came down to the diagnosis of possible allergies to either the detergent I used for washing his coats and bedding or maybe coupled with the gas and cow patty poop, food allergies. So I worked with the vet consistently trying different things and changing things up. All of which I kept track of and journaled.

I was also told to keep Gunner "clean" by regular, twice weekly bathing with special shampoos and skin conditioners. He had a beautiful coat for a Blue Doberman and beautiful skin, not dried out skin which you'd expect with bathing him so often. In fact, with all the bathing, his skin amazed me as where I thought it would dry him out, it seemed the opposite, his skin seemed almost oily if he wasn't bathed twice weekly.

Some shampoos seemed to help but in the end we settled with the best results coming from using "Johnsons Baby shampoo", a good towel dry and then a wipe down with human "Keri" lotion. As he got older, I switched from using the Keri lotion to using a human leave in treatment conditioner called "Infusium". The combination of these two products not only smelled great, but also made Gunner look so nice and shiny. Best of all and most importantly, this left Gunner's coat in amazing condition, something I was always concerned about.

At work, he almost always wore his coat not only because he was cold but I also believed it helped protect him from the dirt of the warehouse. But it was funny, people always said he stank. Not the farting stink which was horrendous but it was like a weird body odor emanating from him. I attributed this to the dusty sort of stale smell of the warehouse and yes, he did stink. You could snuggle or pat him and the smell would be left lingering on your hands until you washed them.

This was another reason why I bathed him so much as the owners had actually commented on it a few times and I didn't want them changing their minds about letting him come to work. Truthfully, I did miss bathing him a few times and his smell became quite offensive in just a few short days.

With the pimples that Gunner consistently had, it seemed to me that because we worked in the warehouse, he must be getting particularly dirty and therefore, his pores were getting clogged and thus leading to his stinky odour.

I always kept in close contact with the vet in regards to these issues and with the pimples at times getting so bad, he was even diagnosed a few times with full blown Puppy Staph infection and had to be treated with actual medication which did take care of the pimples short term. Once he'd finish the meds, he'd have a week or two of clear skin and then they'd come right back again. In the end, the recommendation from the vet was always the same, keep him clean with the regular bathing, so I did.

I got into the habit of bathing Gunner on Tuesdays and Thursdays and brought his bedding home from work on Fridays to be washed and fresh for work on Monday. Add to that, I washed his home bedding also weekly sometimes even more. What I did notice was that every time I bathed him the water was significantly dirty so my theory of it being the warehouse dirt had to be right.

The actual bathing of Gunner I do believe became one of his favorite times as I had always been careful not to get soap in his eyes and always took time to massage him which he enjoyed. He absolutely loved sitting in the tub with the warm water running over him from the shower massager and would even start doing his head bobs as he started to fall asleep.

Gunner's bath time became so routine that no matter where I was in the house that if I said "Bath time", Gunner would jump up and run straight to the tub. When I finally got into the bathroom, he'd be sitting in the tub with this look on his face as if to ask "What took you so long?!?"

Gunner absolutely adored going to work and we adored having him there. The warehouse was over 13,000 square feet, there was simply no way possible to clean this place up more than it was so I adjusted, Gunner had to be bathed and that was that!

When Isaac had passed on and I had finally made the decision of going with the Doberman breed, I had done a list of pros and cons. I remember the definite pros being the amount of time I'd save with the Doberman in vacuuming and grooming.

With Isaac, I had a vacuuming routine of one day ridding the main floor of Isaac hair bunnies and the next day was the upstairs. Five days a week while we watched "Jeopardy", I'd sit on the floor with Isaac sprawled out and I brush him right up until "Final Jeopardy".

With the Doberman not having near the amount hair that the German Shepherd had, I figured the vacuuming and brushing time would be way down. What I didn't factor in were the endless amounts of loads of laundry I did keeping Gunner's fleece and bedding clean. To be honest, he had a heck of a lot more laundry than I did! Add to that the half hour or so every few days it took to change his ear tapes.

Isaac was bathed maybe four times a year, granted it took a long time as I had to blow dry him after but I never imagined bathing a dog twice a week. Gunner didn't need the blow drying as I did vigorously towel dry him after each bath and he did get "bath zoomies" which usually completed his hair dry. But he did love the feel of the hair dryer on him and quite typically interrupted me while I dried my hair after a shower for a quick blast with it. To be honest, I can't remember a time when he didn't interrupt me by nosing me for the hair dryer.

At the end of it all, I didn't regret the accommodations I had to make for Gunner for a second, in fact I treasured every moment of them and it created a very deep bonding.

For a blue Doberman, he actually had an amazing coat for years and numerous other Doberman breeders as well as judges told me this. As stated, he got his Canadian Championship at eighteen months, so his beautiful coat and skin lasted at least until then. But he still got rashes, pimples and shivered a lot and of course, had the terrible room clearing gas.

Above : Gunner trying to cut the lawn for Karen on Calder.
Below : Vegas enjoying the sun on his face.

9 ~ CALDER

When I brought Gunner home his first day, back in March of 2007, I lived in the North End of Winnipeg, Manitoba, Canada and at the time, didn't have a driver's license or vehicle for that matter.

As I started getting involved in showing Gunner, as well as taking him to and from work every day, the cab rides had started to get quite expensive. Because of this, I had decided to take the plunge and get my driver's license and oddly enough, got quite used to driving. I wouldn't say I enjoyed it but it certainly gave me some freedom that I didn't have before.

The house that I had purchased in North End of Winnipeg in 1998 was a relatively large two story house with an adequate sized yard for a city house. I had both a front yard which had one tree in it as well as a good sized back yard. It wasn't in the best of neighborhoods but I was okay with it and dealt with it as it certainly was better than the previous Furby Street area I lived in. But again, it was a rough neighborhood.

Sadly, the house right next to me was a rental and proved to be a real problem house no matter what tenants resided there. There were constant parties and fights which went on to the wee hours of the morning every day of the week. The noise of these parties wasn't such a problem for me because again, I was hearing impaired so for the most part, slept through it all. However other neighbors did take issue to the noise level and did call the police regularly with their concerns.

What I didn't sleep thru though, was the constant lights flashing on the police cruisers that had to attend to the neighbors. This was a constant presence that was always required at the neighbor's house.

I can remember talking to my other neighbor saying that things were getting more and more out of control and if things carried on, there'd be a death before we knew it. Sadly as time went by, things did carry on and the fights did escalate.

I can remember waking up one morning for work and as Gunner and I left, the cops were already at the neighbors. When we came home, there were different cops at the neighbors.

The final week I counted twenty seven different police cruises attending the neighbor's house and again, I was at work every day for eight hours a day. This final week was my deciding factor to consider moving as I just couldn't take it anymore.

Tim says not to say things that you don't want to come true. He says that saying them puts them into action. This was true with my neighbors. Just as I signed the purchase offer on Calder in June of 2008, yet another police cruiser showed up at my neighbors and in no time, so did the coroners van to take away the wife in a body bag. It may be selfish of me, but as I saw the body bag being taken out, I thanked God for me getting out of there.

Mom and dad lived out in the country on a smaller property of land facing a creek in Petersfield, Manitoba just about 40 minutes north of Winnipeg. I had told them it was time for me to move and they agreed to keep an eye out for me on houses in the country. They were the ones that came across the house on Calder as it had a private sale sign that they happened to see on their way home one day, and for that I will be forever grateful.

Calder was amazing! It was an older house built in the early sixties. It was a tiny 980sq foot bi-level house but it was also on five acres of land which would be perfect for the pack of dogs I now had with Gunner, Taxi and Vegas!

The house did have some issues being older but I truly bought it for the land as it was gorgeous with a groomed grass yard and treed with many mature pines, birch and willows as well as many fruit trees.

After living for ten years in the North End, I had equity in that home so with it, I paid off the Escape and still had a healthy deposit for Calder as well as enough money to fence three acres with "wild game fencing" and chain link. I moved in with the pack on a Friday, the fence building party happened that Saturday, and the fence was all up by end of day Sunday! Dad came by to help me with the final touches on Monday and it was then complete. The pack now had three acres of grass and trees to roam in while being safe!

For a dog, particularly a male dog, this yard was complete heaven on earth as there were ample trees to pee on! Poor little Vegas always seemed to not pace himself though and quite commonly ran out of pee before he finished making his rounds. The poor little guy was left to just the grand display of futile leg lifting by the time he reached the final trees in the yard.

Gunner by this time had learned the fine art of mature leg lifting and always started in the reverse direction as Vegas. But Gunner too would eventually run out of pee which I guess in the long run meant that Gunner owned his trees, Vegas owned his trees and then there were some mutually co-owned by the two of them.

I know many people in the country let their dogs roam free but I never felt comfortable with that. I knew there were coyotes around as well as skunks, deer and the highway was only a mile away. Gunner, Taxi or Vegas could get to the highway in no time and I never would have forgiven myself if one of the pack got attacked by a coyote or killed by a car. The fence was great and definitely a peace of mind for me!

Taxi really came into her own on Calder as her terrier hunting skills really kicked in. Calder had a large deck off the back door and Taxi just loved scouring the three acres, attacking and taking her kill under the deck to the area I couldn't reach. She was so good in fact that she actually started having a weight problem from eating her kill. At her yearly vet appointment, it was recommended that I significantly cut down on her food portions because she was obviously getting "natural" supplementation to her diet.

Vegas didn't really show much of a difference on Calder to be honest. He was just Vegas and did his thing. He did teach Gunner how to fetch though and the three of us played this often while Taxi hunted.

Gunner, whom I thought would enjoy the three acres the most actually seemed to have no effect as he always wanted to be within five square feet of me. I guess that's why they commonly refer to Dobermans as "Velcro" dogs.

I had envisioned opening the door and letting the pack out in their huge yard and them frolicking all their energy away. Instead, I'd open the door and Taxi would bolt, with her fluffy ears bouncing in the wind off to the furthest part of the yard to hunt. Vegas would grab the first tennis ball he saw and return and Gunner would have a quick pee and bark at the door like a fool until I either let him in or went out with him.

I loved the yard and the peace that came with it. In total, it was 300 feet across by 700 deep and lined by bushes and trees almost all the way around. The fence was in a "U" shape as the house was on one side, the garage on the other and the driveway was in the center portion. I sat on the deck, in our private little world for hours just watching Taxi hunt and Vegas throw the ball up into the air and catch it.

Gunner, as always, stayed beside me and even got his own chaise lounge with cushion as he refused to just lay on the deck.

I found it truly amazing that there was no police cruisers around, no fighting, swearing or beer bottles strewn about. Not only that, but not once was any of my yard vandalized with gang graffiti or spray painted swear words that to my dismay were even spelt wrong. Out here, I didn't have to chain up my bar-b-que and never did have any of my lawn furniture ever stolen. Best of all, there weren't any stolen grocery carts or garbage strewn about everywhere. I finally had peace and the pack and I loved it!

Gunner and I still went to work every weekday and the drive was also peaceful. In fact, I drove the quite country roads all the way into the city and spent less time on the city roads than before so it was simply perfect! The winter roads proved to be a tad dicey at times but I always kept the shiny side up and the rubber side down on the Escape.

All this yard did have its advantages for sure. I learned quickly that Gunner wasn't burning much energy off sitting beside me all the time so we played fetch a lot to keep him in shape. Gunner's energy typically outlasted my throwing energy so in no time I created an ingenious contraption I referred to as the "Gunner Cuz Sling Shot".

It consisted of two fence posts I hammered into the ground with a sledge hammer about three feet apart from each other. I then took that stupid elastic arm exercising tube thing I'd bought for my arm pit fat and tied it to the posts. But before I tied it to the posts, I cut up one of my white cotton, beat up tube socks and put the elastic thing threw it. In essence, it turned out to be an ugly MacGyvered souped up slingshot that while I sat on the ground, could fire Gunner's favorite toy called a "Cuz" a good hundred and fifty feet or so away!

It didn't work as well for Vegas' tennis balls, but it really sailed that Cuz!

The size of the yard also had more than ample room for Gunner's swimming pool. For the most part yes, he was cold but on those real hot summer days he loved laying in his pool and would do so for upwards of an hour at a time. It looked really comical as in order for him to spend time in his pool, I of course had to move my lawn chair beside him. So I imagine, it could have looked to outsiders that he needed a life guard. I sat there reading and he laid lounging in his kiddie pool.

There were only three times that Gunner really experienced the total size of the yard. That was when he was pooping, marking territory on his trees or when he helped me with the lawn mowing.

I've always prided myself on routine with my dogs and part of routine is scheduled meals. Having a regular schedule for meals typically leads to a regular schedule of pooping. Every morning at wake up and after the pack had their "breakfast", they went outside for their morning poop.

Taxi usually mixed this up with her hunting so she did her business wherever she happened to be at the time.

Vegas was very similar, he would usually go on either his way out to get a tennis ball or on his way back. Gunner, recognizing the stink he caused always went to the furthest tree in the whole yard and went right beside it! This worked fabulous for me because I didn't have to smell it and never had to look for it to clean it up, it was always right by that tree.

When I moved out to Calder, my God mother, Aunty Mildred had offered to give me Uncle Stan's old lawn tractor. This was truly a blessing as I now had a lot of grass to cut on a regular basis and if it wasn't for her, I would have had to do it by hand! Fortunately this also turned into an excellent exercise routine for Gunner.

The Doberman is said to be protective, they were bred for it and it's deep in their genetics. But further to that, the Doberman was meant for "Personal Protection". I say this as my Isaac "worried" about me, the house and whatever was on the street. Whereas Gunner always stayed tight to me and was concerned for me and what was in my personal space it seemed.

I'm not sure if I'm getting the point across at showing the difference in the two. When walking Isaac down the street, he would start to make himself look "big" the minute he saw someone who could be a block away. Whereas Gunner wouldn't make himself look big until that person was within say ten feet of us.

I never trained either Isaac or Gunner to do this per se, due to breeding and genetics, this was instinct.

In the summer time in Manitoba, we get rain, plenty of sunshine and very hot days which are the perfect grounds for grass and weed growing. At Calder, I had to cut the grass at least once a week and sometimes twice.

As I did this, Taxi stayed in front as she learned the noise of the tractor scared mice and frogs which she'd scarf down. After her belly looked like a basketball, she'd go lay down on the deck or in the shade to fend off what I referred to as her "lunch drunk" state.

Vegas would follow with his tennis ball in mouth hoping I'd play fetch. After a few laps he'd give up and join Taxi for a snooze.

Gunner on the other hand jogged beside me for each and every lap no matter how hot or tired he was.

To put the yard size into perspective, the lawn tractor had a bagger that my dad helped me modify for it. When cutting grass, if I bagged it, I usually ended up with approximately ten to twelve large garbage bags when I finished. It was a three to four hour job with just the tractor and another hour or more for the push mower and Gunner stayed in my five square feet the whole way helping me.

Quite commonly when I'd stop the lawn tractor to change or empty the bagger, Gunner would take the time to jump on my lap for a quick snuggle which I absolutely loved. He'd then jump down and as I transferred the bagged grass into the garbage bag, he'd jump back up onto the tractor as if he was going to do the next couple of laps!

The pack and I truly enjoyed this wonderful yard and everything it offered. But there were those few moments when I did look back to the ease of city life and my old small yard.

One bright sunny morning, we had all woken up quite early and after our breakfast and me getting dressed, I let the pack out for their morning constitutional. The minute the door was open, Gunner, Taxi and Vegas bolted for the outside as they so typically did.

As quickly as they bolted out though, I noticed a kerfuffle as Taxi chased something under the deck with great speed. In fear of Taxis' attacking, both Gunner, full grown now and Vegas, before even peeing, sprinted directly back to the door and started howling to come back in. Hearing the commotion, I ran out as I couldn't see Taxi but could hear this crazy screeching and growling coming from under the deck.

As I tried to crawl underneath the deck to rescue my poor little Taxi, to my surprise she came out ever so proudly dragging a rather large rabbit that she killed. This rabbit was almost twice the size of her! I was completely mortified as were Gunner and Vegas!

I had never experienced this before and quite frankly, I was rather taken aback by this horror. I completely understand the circle of life and I get that animals hunt, kill and sometimes eat their kill but my God, Taxi just murdered Peter Cotton Tail.

Not knowing what to do and in somewhat of a panic that all the dogs might try to eat this rabbit now, I ran into the house for a dust pan. Gunner and Vegas still wanted no part of this action but Taxi had scored the mother lode of meals and was bound and determined to protect it.

As I approached Taxi and her kill, she was very reluctant but did move aside from the body rather heart broken. I of course didn't want to touch it so poked it a number of times with the dust pan to insure it was dead. It was definitely dead but as I poked it, the wind would blow its fur making it look like it wasn't.

What was at first my complete mortification quickly turned into fear that this thing might be playing dead and now attack me out of aggression. I quickly scooped up the rabbit in a dustpan that was too small for it and when I tried to toss it over the fence with a quick heave hoe, it landed right dead centre on the hood of my truck.

Now seeing this body on the hood of my truck, Gunner and Vegas being terrified, and Taxi terribly upset for missing out on her meal, all I could think as I started crying was that I hadn't even had my first cup of coffee!

Right or wrong, I left the body where it landed and went inside the house with the pack to try to start our day over. I returned a few hours later to dispose of the body properly by placing it tenderly in a garbage bag, saying a quick prayer and taking it to the dump. But the whole time I replayed the situation in my head. My "Protective Doberman" was terrified of a rabbit and it was my teeny tiny loaf of bread size terrier that violently killed this rabbit. Who would have thought?

As much work as this large property was particularly for me being single, I still enjoyed the peace of it all and never regretted my purchase of Calder for a minute but it was very time consuming hard work! The upside was that it kept me in great condition as well as the whole pack except for Taxi who developed a weight problem.

Sadly, in order to enjoy peace or see the upside of life, you also have to endure the down side and that was coming.

Above : Young Gunner and Vegas playing together.
Below : Young Gunner in the yard snooping with Vegas.

10 ~ BAD ATTITUDE!

From the minute I brought Gunner home, I started raising him into what I thought would be the best dog known to man-kind. I had years of experience with all types of dogs and I'd done various types of training. For anything I felt I was missing in my knowledge, I spent countless hours reading up on. I was so ready for this new puppy and completely had his life scheduled all out and it was a life full of fun and learning.

Everything I had read about Working Dogs and Dobermans in particular stated that consistency, nurturing, having rules and leadership were a must to have a positive relationship with them. I had followed this procedure with Isaac and had never had an issue with him and he had proved the system worked in his fourteen years as he was a very well rounded dog.

Going to work with Gunner, I trained him during breaks in the warehouse, practicing heeling and different commands. At home, we had rules where we sat before we ate, we had manners, and I was the calm pack leader.

I'll be honest, I wasn't strict with Taxi or Vegas as they were pretty small but with Gunner I felt this was really important. I went in the door first and he came second. I would feed him and while he ate, sometimes take up the food dish, interrupting him, and then give it back. He didn't get treats for free, he got dog treats for working and positive reinforcement.

His "bad behavior" wasn't met with a hit or swat but for him, a stern "stop" really took effect. I had learned with the various dogs in my life, by reading countless books and talking to countless dog trainers and owners that each and every dog required something different for learning. There were of course different "methods" of training but not all methods worked for every dog. With Gunner he wanted, for the most part, to please me. If I looked unhappy, he typically picked up on it immediately and stopped whatever he was doing that made me unhappy.

Our "pack" was a happy one! We spent a lot of time outside and even in the winter when a lot of the time outside wasn't an option due to the extreme cold temperatures, we did challenging mental thinking games and obedience in the house for fun.

I had a bedroom upstairs and across the short hallway was the "kennel room / computer room" where Taxi and Vegas slept in their kennels and stayed while Gunner and I were at work.

Beside my bed though, was Gunner's kennel. I'll openly admit, sometimes, particularly when he was young, he'd sleep on the bed with me. But I always insured that he also spent nights in his kennel. To re-affirm who was boss, he was never allowed on the bed until I was already settled in and then I'd call him up. From time to time while on the bed, I would then tell him "off" and he'd jump off and wait until I called him back again.

Sometimes he'd give up waiting and just go curl up in his kennel.

Either way, Gunner, Taxi and Vegas got along really well and other than Taxi being the "fun police" for

Vegas and Gunner every now and then, we lived in complete harmony.

Approximately a month or so after moving to Calder came our first attitude issue. To say "attitude issue" is an understatement, it was a full blown dog fight attack!

I had moved into Calder on July 25th, it was now late August or early September and Gunner was now nineteen months old. I'm still not positive what exactly happened that day but as per normal, we'd all been outside and I'd finished cutting grass with Gunner. We all came into the house and while I made a bee line to the bathroom, the pack moved into the kitchen area.

As I sat down in the bathroom, I heard the most horrific sound ever. The commotion was filled with incredibly loud growling, barking and even a shrill screaming of sorts. There was no doubt in my mind that whatever was going on wasn't good and I had to get there immediately.

I was out of that bathroom in seconds to find Gunner, in the kitchen with Vegas's whole head in his mouth and he was shaking him violently!

I immediately broke up the fight, got Gunner outside and went to inspect Vegas. For lack of a better term, Vegas had a "flip top" head. This is to say that Gunner had torn his scalp right down to his skull from behind his right ear to just above his right eye. The weight of Vegas's ear actually made it so I could see his skull underneath this skin flap and I was mortified!

I put Taxi and Vegas in the bathroom, ran Gunner from outside, up into his kennel and then I was off to the emergency vet where Vegas received almost twenty stiches for his wound.

At the vets', I was sick to my stomach as I relayed everything about Gunner, Vegas and the whole situation that I could to the vet. Gunner had NEVER shown any signs of aggression what so ever to anyone or any of the pack members. He had obedience, he was fed regularly, and we had rules and received regular exercise. I didn't see any food or toys around the area where the fight was and I heard no growling beforehand although with my hearing, I may not have heard if there was growling. Vegas was a very submissive dog and always gave in to Gunner's "leadership". By this time we had established a pecking order in the house and it was me, Taxi, Gunner and Vegas. We were all happy in that order. Vegas was not the type to challenge but again, I didn't see it so couldn't be sure.

Where Gunner had never shown aggression to the pack members, he had recently started to show some aggression to strange dogs. Gunner had gained a lot of socialization at the dog shows from early puppyhood where he was always within close proximity to other dogs. Even with this, Gunner did from time to time raise his hackles at some dogs and he did bark at strange dogs through the truck window. I had noticed that the truck barking wasn't play barking, it was definitely a more serious aggressive barking. But again, he showed none of that to Taxi or Vegas ever.

After discussions, and a full medical examination on Gunner that provided no medical issues, the vet and I could only really come up with two causes.

We had only been at Calder for over a month, so maybe he was under stress from the change that I didn't notice. Gunner was also a maturing intact male meaning he had not been neutered, still had his testicles and was becoming a sexually mature adult.

Either way, Vegas and I headed home. The whole drive I replayed the attack over and over in my head to try to come up with some rational reason for this change in dynamics.

The one thing I noticed was that when I got to the fight, Gunner was not Gunner. I yelled at him, I screamed at him and he didn't hear me. Finally the only way I got him off Vegas was to grab him by the throat from behind, lift him off the ground with Vegas hanging and wait for him to let go of Vegas. I hate to say it, but I think he finally let Vegas go because I was somewhat choking him and this terrified me. There was no doubt in my mind that in that very moment, Gunner wanted Vegas dead and he had zero intentions of stopping until he was.

Dogs fight, it's part of nature and things can happen that cause them to fight. I'd witnessed and even broken up dog fights in the past and typically, when dogs do fight, they stop when one submits. Vegas had peed everywhere and was in complete submission and Gunner didn't stop!

Because I had been so actively involved now with showing Gunner, I had met Mandy, the owner of his father. She was a wonderful lady who lived in North Dakota but came to Winnipeg regularly for various dog shows. We were about the same age and from the minute we met, we had instantly formed a strong friendship.

At that time, Mandy had six Dobermans, she did breed from time to time, and also worked at the SPCA as a kennel technician and even did "temperament testing" on incoming dogs. She was a wealth of knowledge and I knew I now had a problem that I wanted her input on.

I had been in constant contact with her, giving her updates on Gunner, asking for advice in particular with his gas and poop issues and just overall. She had been involved with Dobermans for over fifteen years and "knew" the Doberman breed very well.

When I got home with Vegas, Gunner was left in his kennel and I immediately called Mandy crying.

We talked for hours that night and she had three main conclusions. We had just moved, only been on Calder for just over a month so agreed with the vet that maybe it was the change and it had stressed Gunner and the pack out so that they were behaving differently. Further to that, I was feeling stress with the move and the changes and if the pack didn't, they still would be feeling the stress from me.

The second was, maybe it was over food or toys or behavior referred to as "resource guarding". Gunner had shown with Taxi that he did not appreciate having his bones taken away by her. Granted, he had never growled at her let alone attacked her, but he had shoved the coffee table at her on numerous occasions. He was nineteen months now and "maturing" so maybe his level of dealing with toys or bones being taken away was getting more intense. The good news was, I had addressed the situation immediately and by the yelling, grabbing and putting Gunner outside, had shown that it was un-acceptable behavior.

Lastly but most importantly, Mandy said that maybe it could be medical and perhaps the vet had missed a sore spot. Maybe Gunner had hurt himself outside and had lashed out at Vegas due to some unseen pain. But more importantly, Mandy raised the common problem of Hypothyroidism as Dobermans had a strong tendency to have thyroid issues. She had seen aggression with dogs that were not properly treated for Hypothyroidism.

The phone call ended with me now booking an appointment for Gunner with his "normal" vet, the vet who knew his complete health history but who also knew me historically and how I raise my dogs. In the meantime, I'd watch the interactions in the house a lot closer.

The next day in the vets' office with Gunner was surreal. The vet knew our house and the rules we had, he knew the training we did and the exercise that the pack all received. As I spoke, I saw the dis-belief in his eyes. And how could he not be in disbelief? Gunner, like normal at his vet visits was having a great time. It was like nothing had ever happened with him!

He checked Gunner over physically and he showed no signs of tenderness anywhere. He listened to his heart, checked his teeth and poked and prodded him but Gunner showed nothing.

I discussed what Mandy had said about the whole thyroid thing and the vet looked at Gunner and openly stated it wasn't thyroid. Thyroid showed by laziness, the dog being overweight or having a really poor coat. And yes, it was prominent in the Doberman breed but usually didn't display until they were five years or older. Gunner didn't show any of these symptoms. Gunner was the complete opposite of all these symptoms being in excellent condition, excellent weight, very active and had a remarkable coat. The only issues Gunner had was gas, cow patty poop and what we felt was allergies and the occasional staph infection.

I asked that the vet test him anyways for thyroid as Mandy had insisted so strongly. His reply was that it was money I was flushing down the toilet and simply no point. So I believed him, he was the vet!

He did state that Gunner was used to a very set schedule with me all his life and moving to Calder was change that quite possible stressed him out. The vet also knew Vegas and since Isaac had passed, he felt Vegas was overly submissive. This coupled with Gunner "maturing" may have been the opportune time for Gunner to "advance" in the packs pecking order. This may have been a display of dominance albeit a rather aggressive one.

So, the vet had recommended that we "keep an eye on it" and see what happens.

For the next few days, I re-introduced Gunner back into the pack with Taxi and Vegas very slowly and very controlled. I watched for posturing in the dogs when they passed each other or were in close proximity to each other. I strategically started to place toys and bones around them and watched for the resource guarding.

I literally followed these dogs now around the house and yard and spent hours just watching them even for the most subtle of dirty looks or what I have always called "stink eye" towards each other. Truthfully, they were all back being happy as larks.

It took Vegas the longest to relax but I could understand that. He healed perfectly but you could see he was nervous of Gunner now, and for the first week or so seemed to be watching over his shoulder to keep an eye on Gunner. This however may have been advantageous as maybe I had miss-read the pecking order and maybe Gunner was establishing the new order.

Either way, Vegas soon seemed to let this go as well and started playing again with Gunner.

For Gunner, he seemed to completely forget about the whole situation by the next day and acted as he always did. Gunner was a very snuggly, obedient dog who enjoyed playing with Vegas and following Taxi.

For me, I had difficulties forgetting the attack so continued to watch them all like hawks!

I was surrounded by dog people now from the dog show world daily and had many conversations with a variety of people in regards to this attack. It bothered me to my core as I'd never in my life experienced anything like this. I'd never seen a dog not stop fighting and seem to have such a "kill" face on him.

As much as I hated talking about the situation, I talked about it anyways because I still didn't understand the "why" behind it. As much as I appreciated the input from others, most people came back with the same cautions, maybe I was too lenient on Gunner, maybe he wasn't trained well enough. Maybe there weren't enough rules in the house and now Gunner thought he was the boss. Many people commented on how I let him on the furniture and even my bed, they felt that Gunner was coddled and now spoiled.

I couldn't see these as issues though, I had spent more time training and working with Gunner than all my other dogs including Isaac combined. Yes, he was allowed on the furniture but that came with rules that I exercised all the time. I would make him wait until I told him he could jump up. I'd regularly tell him "beep beep" which meant to move for me even though I didn't need him to but he'd quickly get out of my way.

Some people recommended me training Gunner with a "firmer hand" and using compulsion training or even swatting. I have always believed in the purpose of compulsion training in certain circumstances but also have always said that each dog needs different things. Gunner listened very well to me and didn't need a hard correction on a choke chain to do it.

Back in the day of Isaac, I had occasion to take him to an obedience class with a trainer that said compulsion training was physical training. It was his opinion that where it had its place particularly in the foundation of training, one had to recognize that if you had to control a dog with physical touch then the minute that dog was out of reach you would lose that control and the dog would know it.

His classes had all the dogs on leash but he showed us ways to train that would gain mental control of the dogs instead, The leashes were for minimal use and primarily to keep the dog from wandering off in the beginning of training.

For an example, the classic exercises we did regularly was to put the dogs in a down stay and place treats or their toys out of reach. The dog was not to take the treat without the handler giving the "take it" command. The treat or toy was closer to the dog then the handler. We also did heeling where the leash was hanging loose over our shoulder as opposed to in our hand. If the dog wandered, we could take the leash but it wasn't for a correction.

I had practiced this type of training with Gunner regularly and he excelled at it. I could place Gunner in a sit, put a treat on his nose, and with Taxi and Vegas wandering around him, I could leave the room. Minutes later I would return and come back to see drool hanging from the sides of Gunner's mouth and he'd be starring cross eyed at the treat. But he wouldn't take it until I gave the word.

While I could appreciate what others were saying about Gunner thinking he ruled the roost, I just couldn't see it. I will admit though, he was stubborn and had attitude but I always insured I won the battle!

I continued my regular phone calls with Mandy to talk about how the pack was interacting in their daily routine. Where Mandy was cautious, she concurred with me that quite possibly this was an isolated incidence that I had addressed quickly so therefore was now a dead issue.

Mandy was however saddened that I hadn't followed through with the thyroid test and did mention getting the test done a few times just to eliminate it as a contributing factor. But the pack was doing well, we all were and seemed to be back to being very happy again.

Over the course of the next few weeks and into the following month, slowly, Gunner gained back my trust and we were back to being the happy family enjoying the country life and all the peace it offered. I did however, increase Gunner's Obedience training just to insure that he knew who was boss. This was also the contributing factor to Gunner and I getting involved in Rally Obedience.

Above : Puppy Blaze and Taxi checking out Calder.
Below : Blaze pictured at approximately 2 years old.

11 ~ DADDY'S LITTLE GIRL

Mandy and I would talk multiple times a week about our dogs and our lives. We became long distance friends. I don't think I ever told her and hope she reads this here, but I have a very great respect for her!

She had a beautiful female Doberman named Chana that she had decided to breed. With all her research, she had finally picked what she felt was a suitable male from New York that she would breed her with. Mandy had a very nice red male Doberman in her house but as good breeders do, she looked for the best breeding match as opposed to the easiest or most convenient match.

Chana was both a Canadian and American Champion red female that didn't carry the dilution gene and the male was an American Champion, black and tan that also didn't carry the dilution gene. If the breeding took, Mandy would only have black or red puppies based on the colour genetics of the sire and dam.

During our conversations, she gave me updates on the whole procedure like the progesterone testing on Chana to see if she was ready for breeding. She told me of the travel plans to New York and the actual breeding itself in great detail and I enjoyed hearing and learning about it.

Obviously, I knew that dogs bred and puppies were typically the results of breeding but Mandy and I spent hours talking about lineages, physical traits, health testing and pedigrees. This was no, find another Doberman and let the two of them go at it. This was science, research, and full preparation and care taken in the hopes of insuring a healthy litter born from a healthy mom. This litter was created in the hopes that each and every puppy would strongly represent the breed of Doberman in all of its finest qualities and attributes.

After the breeding had taken place, Mandy had multiple exams, ultrasounds and x-rays done by her vet to keep an eye on the actual pregnancy and the puppies. Just like with a human pregnancy, Mandy even got a printed copy of one of the tests and together we tried to count the itty bity skeletons to try to determine how many puppies Chana was carrying. The count, though it would not be 100% accurate would at least inform Mandy of what to prepare for. Surprising to me, even after the mom finished labor, she was x-rayed again to insure that no puppies were left inside that could cause possible health complications with infections for the mom.

Mandy did everything possible and then more when it came to breeding and I learned so much. I still had no interest in breeding, but this was confirmed even more as I learned by her example. It became obvious, to breed properly and ethically, it was darned hard work and expensive!

I can remember during this time, out of curiosity I asked Mandy if she spent so much on all this, how much money did she actually think she'd make? Quickly Mandy burst out in laughter and said, "If you breed Dobermans properly, you typically lose money and sometimes you're lucky enough to break even."

Many may not believe this but let's take a second to break down the "costs", as I'm a numbers person. To start, there is the cost of your dog, in Mandy's case, the female; the cost of training, feeding, vetting and extra testing for possible diseases. Also, hip and elbow x-rays and holter monitors for Cardio testing. And then literally thousands of dollars for showing in dog shows to "prove" that your female meets the breed standards. You can save costs by showing your dog yourself instead of hiring a professional handler but you still incur costs when you travel for shows such as hotel, gas, and eating out in restaurants.

Then in Mandy's case, she chose a male to breed with that she didn't own so there were stud fees with the breeding. Before the breeding there were medical exams on Chana to insure she was fit for breeding, and then the related progesterone testing alerting Mandy of when she was ready to be bred.

For the breeding alone, Mandy incurred travel costs to take Chana to the male, more hotel and eating out costs while on route and while breeding. Believe it or not, this wasn't a one-time breed and leave. Typically you do two or three breedings to increase your chances of it taking and you do the breeding days apart. During this time, there was also a loss of wages for Mandy missing work. All of these costs still did not guarantee that the litter would take though!

So after the breeding and the travelling back home, then came the costs to insure that Chana was pregnant. More costs were incurred during the pregnancy to keep Chana healthy and follow the puppies' growth. Finally, the litter was born and then came the vet costs of the exams for the puppies to insure their health. Added to that, with the puppies maintaining their health there were extra costs to have their tails docked by the vet as well as the costs for traveling to get their ears done by yet another vet. This meant yet another loss of wages while Mandy traveled and missed work again.

It was evident to me that this was not done to get rich, but again, Mandy spared no expenses because she had hopes of furthering the Doberman breed.

During this time, Mandy had started somewhat joking to see if I would consider taking another puppy and every time it came up, I flatly said no. I already had a house chalk full of three trouble makers. But I have to admit, the thought of another puppy was sure exciting especially since I now had it all "figured out" and had done so well by Gunner.

Chana delivered her puppies on August 10th, 2008 and had a very healthy litter of mostly black and tan puppies but a few reds puppies speckled the litter.

Mandy told me about the pups as they grew and she interviewed perspective owners diligently. Some she turned down and others excited her and she deemed them to be either great pet homes or show homes.

When the litter was about five or six weeks old, Mandy drove with the whole litter to Kentucky to have the puppies evaluated by her mentor, a fellow Doberman lover and professional handler. It was here that her mentor would advise her which puppies she thought to be closer to standard than others. This, along with temperament would help Mandy to decide which puppies were available for show homes or pet homes.

As well, she also had the puppy's ears cropped by a gentlemen who was not only a certified long time vet but who was known amongst Doberman breeders to do amazing crops.

By the time Mandy got home, as is common with all good breeders, she had more homes than puppies.

A week before Chana's puppies started to go to their respective homes, one of the "show home" people canceled and Mandy was now left with her second pick, a little black female available. Mandy was already keeping the pick of the litter but she wanted her second pick to go somewhere special. She wanted her second pick to also be shown as well as be a loved family pet and taken care of.

I still remember the day quite vividly.

I was sitting at my desk at work when Mandy called and DEMANDED that I check my email as she had something very important for me to see. When I opened up the email there were the most gorgeous big black eyes looking at me almost upside down!

I'll never forget that picture. There was a big wood box with all the puppies in it, all wearing their different colored collars for identification. There was one puppy hanging half out, "high centered" on the plywood looking like she was ready to face plant onto the linoleum on the other side. This was her "trouble maker second pick girl".

When I called Mandy, there was no "hello" just a simple, "She can be yours, just say the word!"

This was only two months after the horrifying episode between Gunner and Vegas. But, there hadn't been another one like it. No squabbles, no growls or even dirty "stink eye" looks. Mandy and I discussed it regularly. It truly seemed to be a "one of" situation that had been vigorously addressed and had never happened since.

Calder had a huge yard, great for dogs, it's not like I didn't have room. And I showed dogs, albeit first with a professional handler but by that time, I had been showing Gunner in Conformation by myself. For both Mandy and I, this was a perfect situation and so the deal was done!

Before I knew it, this time mom, dad and I were driving to the Canada and US border to meet my new little girl! I did have my own Escape still, but I wanted to hold her on the way back and do that snuggling that Gunner and I had when I brought him home.

We met Mandy and my cute little "Blaze" at the US and Canadian border, talked for a few minutes then jumped right back into our vehicles and off we went to head home with the newest pack member!

Gunner and Blaze immediately proved to be different. Whereas Gunner slept in my arms so lovingly and peacefully on the way home, Blaze screeched at the top of her lungs and wouldn't sit still! Further to that, we stopped for pee breaks that she didn't use to her fullest potential and ended up peeing on my lap.

Needless to say, when we finally got home, I stank, had a splitting head ache and was totally exhausted.

Blaze's kennel was set up in the kennel room between Vegas and Taxi. Although everyone in our home loved their kennels, Blaze hated every minute of it. She howled until she cried herself to sleep and in the morning, the second she awoke she howled some more.

I didn't run to the kennel to rescue her because I knew if she got her way, it would only get worse but in the morning she would get so mad that the howling would turn to bear stomping and within minutes that puppy that had box cutter blades for teeth would shred every piece of blanket or soft toy she had.

So, two Dobermans, opposite end of the spectrum. Valuable lesson learned.

Where Gunner and Blaze were so different, they both still had strong drive and learning capabilities. Gunner liked direction from me but Blaze didn't need anybody's help nor anyone telling her what to do. Where Gunner needed my support the first time to investigate a full garbage bag, Blaze shredded it and its contents before I could turn around. Blaze was true to that picture of her hanging upside down half over the board, she was scared of nothing and needed nobody!

I'll be honest, I was real nervous with this little girl on fire! True to her name "Blaze", she left a path of unrecognizable destruction after she'd been somewhere and was always in some kind of trouble. The blessing was, she fit into the pack famously and we were harmonious in our living, not as peaceful as we once were due to her constant vocals. But we were harmonious and I was hearing impaired so it did work.

Blaze and Taxi hit it off right from the start as even though Blaze needed no one, she still liked company while she investigated every corner of the three acre yard. While Taxi hunted, Blaze shredded.

When I had purchased Calder I had immediately started to make it my own. Dad and I had gone to the local garden shop and I purchased two lovely plum trees, two crab apple trees, six Russian Lilacs, four Forsythia bushes as well as many other miniature Lilacs and planted them all strategically throughout the yard. I could hardly wait to see the fruit of my labor pay off!

In one short month of Blaze being with us, she had shredded all but one of the Russian Lilacs, all but one of the miniature Lilacs and had significantly damaged one of the plum trees. Please don't think for a second that I simply just threw the dogs in the yard for hours at a time by themselves. I watched them all but Blaze was amazing at sneaking off and shredding!

Fortunately, Blaze never ate what she shredded for the most part but picking up her poop proved to be quite entertaining as you could often see just a slight resemblance of what trouble she had gotten into the day before.

Blaze's favorite time in the house was when I went to the bathroom as she quickly learned that for the next three minutes she could engage in unbridled destruction.

In the living room I had two large book cases filled with all kinds of books as I loved to read and was always eager to learn new things. For the first little while, every bathroom break I took resulted in the tragic loss of one of my books. My breaking point was when I came out to find Shakespeare's "Merchant of Venice" shredded all over the living room. The next day in Blazes poop, I found a little piece of paper that you could even still make out "the quality of mercy is not strained, it droppith" and it broke my heart. From that point on, Blaze joined me in the bathroom and it drove her nuts.

They say if you don't want your dogs to take things, then to make sure you don't leave them on the dog shelf. This is completely true but with Blaze that meant from the floor to five feet up. The average counter height in a home falls under that five feet. The stove, kitchen cabinets, kitchen table, and fridge door handle all fall under that five foot line.

The only drawback about the Calder home was that it was built during the era of having multiple small rooms as opposed to the now "open concept" layouts.

When you came in the back door you were immediately facing the bathroom and stairs to go up to the second floor. To your immediate left was the kitchen that had on one side the dining room and my office. If you went through the kitchen and then through the dining room, you were in the tiny but long living room.

For Blaze and her lightning speed, this worked fabulously for her destructive tendencies. I would be sitting on the couch in the living room settled in to watch television and she'd jump up and bolt. By the time I found her, which was within seconds, the destruction was typically done and that precious little puppy would be sitting in the middle of it so terribly proud of herself.

Looking back, I remember Mandy saying that this litter was a "busy" litter and I never asked her what that actually meant. I know now that it meant these puppies were crazy active and adventurists! To this day, I don't remember Blaze sleeping as a puppy whereas Gunner loved his little naps. As I look back at all my dog pictures, not one is of Blaze sleeping soundly, the pictures I have of Blaze are all riddled with destruction.

This "busy" litter proved very true as most of the puppies at one time or another required emergency vet visits. In fact, I think Blaze was the only one who didn't surprisingly enough.

Her one sister at thirteen months had decided that she really didn't like the owners' quarter horse. Biding her time, she waited until one night when the owner wasn't watching and she bee lined to horses paddock where she bit off a little more than she could chew. She picked a scrap with that horse and ended up with a $5,000.00 vet bill for hip surgery when she lost.

Blazes brother ended up at 10 months having a $1,500.00 obstruction surgery for getting into the bathroom cupboard and eating a box of feminine products that expanded rapidly in his stomach.

Another one of Blazes brothers opted to eat patio stone as a snack. I don't mean gravel, I mean he started to chow down on an actual patio block, the kind that measures 12" by 24". How he broke that patio stone up and not his teeth we never did figure out. He ended up with a $1,500.00 obstruction surgery to remove the broken chunks that he didn't pass in his stool.

But my all-time favorite was the puppy that Mandy kept back as her "pick".

As Mandy and her husband stood at the kitchen sink doing dishes one night with their Dobermans playing in the yard, Mandy noticed Blaze's sister go flying by the window, dragging something with all the Dobermans chasing behind her. They were mortified to see that she had ripped an eight foot piece of siding off their new home.

So I guess at the end of the day, I was pretty darn lucky with Blaze!

Putting aside the destruction, attitude and trouble, Blaze was an adorable puppy and I couldn't help but love her! Where Blaze was in trouble most of the time, to me, this showed feistiness, strength, determination, intelligence and I was eager to start working that puppy! A lot of trainers will get excited with puppies like this as once you can direct that energy, you can really end up with a strong working partner.

I realize now that even though they were both Dobermans, there were significant differences in Gunner and Blaze. Blaze didn't suffer from that terrible gas that still plagued Gunner. Her stool was easy to pick up, and rarely smelled which I found quite miraculous given the things she did eat that she shouldn't have. Blaze also didn't have that body odor that Gunner did, the rashes or the pimples and she rarely was bathed. I mentioned this too to the vet and he felt they were just simply different dogs. I agreed and did believe that all dogs were different but it still seemed odd to me.

The one thing I significantly missed though, was Blaze wasn't a snuggly or affectionate puppy. Blaze could not stand to be held and as much as I'd try to pick her up, she'd squirm and struggle to get free as she had always had something more important to do it seemed.

Gunner, on the other hand, would sit right beside me and even on my lap as an adult at 90lbs and longed to snuggle whereas Blaze was more the kind to sit at the opposite side of the couch. She didn't seek out patting and attention from me like Gunner did but I grew to appreciate and accept that. That was just my little Blaze, too busy for love!

Little did I know, Blaze just needed her Tim! With him, her world would change and together both Blaze and Tim would change.

Soon enough, Blaze would become Daddy's little girl and love every minute of it!

Above : Taxi in her early teens at Calder.
Below : Gunner and Karen snoozing after a hard day's work.

12 ~ DOING YOUR DUE DILIGENCE

The one thing I always liked about buying a dog from a good breeder was that if you do your due diligence and research, you know what you're getting. I've said repeatedly in this book that a good breeder tries to achieve the breed standards in every way, so therefore, their puppy is literally born with a job that's genetically predetermined and has been proven time after time and generation after generation.

I will make a statement next that many will jump to judgement on, but I hope that you'll read through this chapter to understand and see my complete reasoning.

Pure bred dogs from good breeders are different than rescue dogs, cross bred dogs or "backyard" bred dogs whether they're pure bred or crosses.

I stand here and say, I do not believe one life is more "valuable" than another or that one dog deserves more love, affection and caring than another. A pure bred dog does not have more value of life than a rescue or cross bred dog.

I don't stand on my soap box saying "buy only pure bred dogs from good breeders". But I will stand on my soap box, fist in the air and yell that whatever choice you make, realize that you are making a commitment for that animals life. If you do not do your due diligence, you may have a very difficult time living up to that lifetime commitment.

I feel, that dogs, all dogs, are truly happiest when doing their job. I don't mean necessarily in a hardworking serious nature but in a fun, together, owner and dog relationship.

I've known a few teachers and they say the biggest thrill for them is when they find out what a students' talent is and they can assist in nurturing that. They say the excitement in the student is what validates what it means to them to be a teacher. This, I find is the same for dogs, being able to nurture them and their instinct, in what comes natural to them.

If you take Taxi for example, the dog I ran over in a cab and kept, she was a cross between some form of terrier and some other small dog. She was scruffy with a brown, grey and black course but yet somewhat smooth coat. I guessed and the vet concurred that she possibly had some Yorkshire Terrier as well as some Border Terrier in her.

If you read the CKC or AKC breed standards for the Yorkshire Terrier, you'll learn that the breed was developed in the 19th century in Yorkshire, England. The breeds' "job" was to catch rats in the clothing mills during this time. Their life span is said to be between thirteen and twenty years of age.

If you read the CKC or AKC standards on the Border Terrier, they state that the Border Terrier was bred as a fox and vermin hunter and its origin is from Scotland / England areas. They too, have a long lifespan.

That fateful day I took Taxi in and for the years I lived in the city with a small yard, I never did do any research on Taxi's breeds, or on what Taxi's natural "job" was. What she displayed was a very happy go lucky, snoopy, scrappy little dog. I do believe she was very happy in the city and enjoyed her life there. Having said that, she always wanted more yard. I say this as she was an absolute brilliant escape artist and it would bring me to tears each and every time she got out.

The yard in the North End was completely fenced with chain link right to the ground but because of Taxi, each gate had either planks of plywood or cement blocks covering the spaces where the gates and fence met. If these spaces were not covered, I'd spend hours chasing that little girl around the neighborhood. Further to that, I had to consistently do perimeter checks to insure I got her "dig spots" which she strategically started by the fence lines.

While Taxi was happy, unbeknownst to me, she was constantly trying to increase her "hunting grounds". The minute she was released in the three and a half acre yard on Calder, she exploded into her greatness!

By the time I moved to Calder, Taxi was approximately ten years old and she lasted to be about seventeen years old. But to see her during this time was amazing and a complete joy! It was almost as if she got younger moving out to Calder. The more she hunted and killed, the happier she was and more behaved in the house. I do believe this is because she was not only allowed to follow her instincts but I also nurtured it!

I never scolded her for her for hunting and killing, and please don't think for a second that I enjoyed it. It was disgusting and at times heartbreaking but it was her nature. I'm not a vet and have never claimed to be, but I do think Taxi lived to be seventeen because she was allowed to follow her instincts and live as the dog she was supposed to be.

Please don't misunderstand me here, I'm not saying your terrier needs to hunt and kill to be happy or that your tiny terrier needs three and half acres to run. There are many terriers that live in the city that live very long happy lives in apartments with loving owners! But what I am saying is, for me, I love to get into the heads of dogs and it was amazing to see her change and grow.

Also, reading and understanding what her breed was bred for helped to explain Taxi and her various behaviors. What I find sad is, I never really read up on her possible breeds until after moving to Calder. Had I learned earlier, it would have explained a lot to me as well as spared me some tears. Further to that, I could have made her life even better!

The hardest thing for me was Taxi always wanting to run away from home. I took this incredibly personal as I felt the classic "I cook for you, I clean for you and this is how you treat me?" None of my other dogs ran away, because they loved me so much. But Taxi MUST have hated me, because in my mind, she was always looking for a way out.

After learning and gaining more understanding of her breeds, I learned that love had nothing to do with it. Her escaping was part of her nature, she was hunting and she was naturally "going to ground" with her trying to dig out.

Her nature was also what made her a better house mouser than any cat I'd ever seen!

Why am I discussing this so much? Who cares? A dog is a dog is a dog right?

The more time I spent in the "dog world" with showing and training, I also got involved with the rescue world. Truth be told, for a number of years, dogs were my life, every kind of dog. I loved "talking dogs", would do it for hours, enjoyed it and I was good at it. I loved learning about all dogs! I truly found them all to be amazing creatures.

I can remember at work one day a client had come in to purchase something and of course was greeted by Gunner. After some Gunner related discussion, he asked me to find a home for his family dog as the dog had bitten his young child twice now and his wife said she had to go because she was a danger and couldn't be trusted. I started asking questions because a dog biting children was very serious and truthfully doesn't have much of a future.

The dog was a female Border Collie whom was four years old, spayed, had regular vet visits and was raised by them as a puppy with their child. The child was a five year old little boy who loved the dog as she was his best friend.

The two times the dog had bitten the child had occurred in the exact same scenario. Each time, the dog had bitten the little boy on the backside of his ankle or lower leg and each time it happened, the parents were on the deck and the little boy was at the utmost back part of their yard.

For those reading who know Border Collies and their jobs, you're probably screaming the answer out or the "why" to this serious situation.

If we refer to the CKC or AKC standards and read other references of the Border Collie we learn that the craft of tending flocks of sheep was introduced to the British by the Romans and it wasn't long before Celtic clans developed their own types of sheepdogs to tend to these tasks. The Border Collie is one of these breeds and is recognized as one of the finest sheep-herding dogs in the world!

So, put the parents on the deck, the five year old at the back of the yard, farthest away from the parents and what you get is a dog doing its job and trying to herd that little boy back to the parents. Further to that, often while herding, the Border Collie will use many tactics to move it's "stock". It will crouch and stare, it will chase and drive and yes, it may nip at the stock in an effort to direct its movement.

This was my guess based on the limited knowledge I had on border collies. I recommended that the man and his wife consult with their breeder, other people and their vet before doing anything hasty but it was my humble opinion.

Months later, the customer came back and reported that he and his wife had consulted others as well as their vet and everyone had felt the same thing. They stopped putting the dog in that position with the child and never had a problem again. Further to that, they took the dog to "herding classes" and their dog not only excelled but got much needed exercise and the whole family really enjoyed it!

This, to me, is the epitome of doing your research and making sure you get a dog that fits your family. But further to that, knowing your dog and it's "job" can also help with troubleshooting issues that come up as well as help you raise the happiest, healthiest dog possible.

The Canadian Kennel Club and the American Kennel Club recognize pure bred dogs. They have taken every one of the recognized pure bred dogs and placed them into one of seven groups based on each breeds' "job".

The CKC currently recognizes 175 breeds in total and each of these breeds are placed into one of these seven groups; Sporting Dogs, Hounds, Working Dogs, Terriers, Toys, Non-Sporting Dogs and Herding. The AKC does differ slightly from this, having said that, being a Canadian resident, going forward I'll address the CKC only.

Group one of the CKC is the Sporting Dog Group and covers, but is not limited to, the following popular breeds such as Pointers, Retrievers, Setters, Spaniels, Vislas and Wiemeraners. For the most part, all of the

Sporting Dog breeds are bred to employ some type of tactic to flush out and retrieve game birds.

Group two of the CKC is the Hound Group and covers, but is not limited to, the following popular breeds such as Afghans, Basset Hounds, Irish Wolfhound, Pharoah Hound, Rhodesian Ridgeback, Dachshunds, and Whippets. The hound group is split into two factions – those long-limbed canines that hunt by sight and those dogs that hunt by scent.

Group three of the CKC is the Working Dog Group and covers, but is not limited to, the following popular breeds such as Akitas, Boxers, Dobermans, Great Danes, Mastiffs, Newfoundlands, Rottweilers, Saint Bernards, Samoyeds and Siberian Huskys. The breeds in the working group all have some specific job to do such as pull sleds, or carts while other breeds in this group guard livestock, homes, businesses or even military installations.

Group four of the CKC is the Terrier Group and covers, but is not limited to, the following popular breeds such as Border Terriers, Cairn Terriers, Fox Terriers, Kerry Blue Terriers, Manchester Terriers and Wheaton Terriers. The Latin word "terra" means ground and thus comes the name of the terriers as an appropriate description for dogs bred specifically to "go to ground" or dig after vermin and small game.

Group five of the CKC is the Toy Group and covers, but is not limited to, the following popular breeds such as Cavalier King Charles Spaniel, Chihuaua, Griffon, Havanese, Maltese, Pekinese, Pomerainian, Poodle, Pug and Yorkshire Terrier. The toy group covers a variety of breeds specifically bred to decimate rodent population while other breeds in this group were bred primarily as pampered lap dogs.

Group six of the CKC is the Non-Sporting Dog Group and covers, but is not limited to, the following popular breeds such as American Eskimo, Bichon Frise, Chinese Shar-Pei, Dalmation, Keeshound, Lhasa Apso, Poodle (miniature and Standard). When a particular breed didn't quite seem to fit in one of the other six groups, it became part of the non-Sporting Group. This isn't to say they don't have jobs, as each of these breeds are in fact very unique but the more that you understand of each of these breeds, you being to understand the rationale.

Group seven of the CKC is the Herding Dog Group which covers, but is not limited to, the following popular breeds such as Australian Cattle Dog, Bearded Collie, Border Collie, Briard, German Shepherd, Old English Sheepdog, Welsh Corgi, and Shetland Sheepdog. In essence, each breed of herding dogs is bred to control a variety of livestock and all herding dogs have been developed to be well suited for their special functions.

Earlier in this chapter I stated "Pure bred dogs from good breeders are different then rescue dogs, cross bred dogs or "backyard" bred dogs." This is where I explain.

I have often used the term "good" breeders, and I explained this as people who have studied their breed of choice. They've done research on their breed and chosen two dogs to breed in order to get as close as possible to the standards set out by a National recognized board. They do their health tests in order to attempt to eradicate certain genetic issues or diseases. They attempt to improve the health quality of their breed. All of this is because they love their breed of choice.

Rescue dogs are that, they typically come from circumstances that require their rescuing. They may come from deplorable conditions of filth and disease. They may come from seizures of hoarding where they saw no vetting and were products of severe malnourished parents. They may come from areas where simply feral dogs run rampant and breed indiscriminately.

"Back yard" bred dogs are that, these dogs are typically products of people who care nothing about what they are breeding but simply the dollar value they can generate by reproducing two dogs. This may result in what they call "pure bred dogs" but they typically do zero health testing or zero training with their dogs because simply, that costs money and results in less profit. These puppies may also fall under the "Designer Dog" category.

Cross bred dogs or "Designer dogs" are a different group altogether. These are sometimes two pure bred dogs of different breeds, bred together to create a "new" or "designer" breed. Sometimes, these people might do health testing and might do training but the resulting puppies are still cross bred dogs albeit sometimes better care is taken.

Okay, so now who's reading this with anger in them, wondering who the hell I am to say one is better than the other? Well then you've jumped to conclusions as I think no such thing! But all of this is important to understand if you're truly doing your due diligence.

The point I make is, and I repeat, the Canadian Kennel Club as well as the American Kennel Club have listed recognized breeds. This means that those two governing bodies have recognized a breed. They do this by a breed proving consistency in its "standards" not over a year or so but for many years, decades in cases.

Let's go back to the Doberman for example now. The Doberman is a recognized breed by the CKC and has been for many years. It has standards that state what a Doberman should be in all areas. When I read the standards on the Doberman, I chose that breed because of what that little puppy should be. I then went to a good breeder and got my puppy!

Taxi was a rescue cross dog or what they used to call back in the day, a mutt. I have no idea what her breeding was or where she came from other than she was malnourished and running the streets of the North End of Winnipeg. At the time that I ran over her in the cab, I simply grabbed her up and rushed her to the vet. She was dirty, stank, matted and as I said, malnourished so she needed "rescuing"! She had no tattoo or microchip, collar or any tags. Based on all of this, I made an assumption that she was a rescue situation and I rescued her.

I absolutely adored her, Vegas and Gunner! But I also had no idea where she came from, how old she was or what she would "bring to the table" in the years to come.

Where the vet and I guessed at her breeds, I still was never sure. I also never knew what possible diseases she may have over the course of her life. I didn't even know how to groom her properly. But yes, I did figure it out and I did love her to bits! She was never less or more important than Gunner or any other dog I ever had. Part of the reason why I loved her so much was in fact because I believed I rescued her.

Having said that, over the years, she proved many things one of which is she loved to try to escape. Even though she had an amazing home, she would try to escape.

I could brush her for hours and once she jumped off my lap and shook her hair, she looked a complete mess again.

Because of her attitude, she was always dirty and stinky. She absolutely adored rolling in "dead things" right after I bathed her.

After getting to know Taxi, I often wondered, did I actually rescue her? Or did she previously live with a loving family albeit in a crappy neighborhood and simply go on a hunting extravaganza which left her lost? This was something that as time went by with Taxi always ached in my heart. When Taxi came into my life, I didn't know her story, I made assumptions because I knew nothing about her.

Rescues, cross breeds and "back yard" bred dogs, you don't know their story. You may think you know but you don't. This doesn't make them less valuable or less worthy of love, it just means you may need to learn more and it may take time. I believe you should want to learn more for these dogs and you should want to take that time.

Here's where I go back to doing your research and finding the dog that fits your family whether it's a pure bred from a good breeder, a rescue or what have you. Any of these can make amazing family members and all of them deserve to have owners commit to them. If your dog has five breeds in him or her, read up on all five breeds!

Here's my next story, one of due diligence not done and the ramifications.

I remember the phone call of a very excited owner who had just put a deposit $500.00 on a "pure bred mini-labradoodle". She was so excited about her new puppy, she wanted to find out immediately who could put in a two foot fence all the way around her yard and thought I might know someone. My first question was "why only a two foot fence?" and her reply was that the breeder said she wouldn't need anything else and she could easily step over that.

Politely I started asking if she had done her due diligence on this "breeder". She truly believed she had. The woman had a beautiful house and seemed to know a lot about the "breed". The breeder would give the puppy her shots and she even had the registered papers from the CKC showing that the parents were pure bred.

Sadly, the mother was in fact a registered Labrador and the father was in fact a registered small Poodle. The "breeder" was what I refer to as a backyard breeder or Designer Dog breeder. She used perfect buzz words to sell this puppy for maximum profit. And actually, the cost of this puppy was more than an actual pure bred Labrador or pure bred Poodle!

With this excited woman I explained the purpose of the CKC and that they did not recognize "mini-labradoodles. But they did recognize Poodles and Labradors. Based on the "standards" of the two breeds, the Labrador for example could grow to easily step over a two foot fence so I would recommend highly on getting a five foot fence.

I remember vividly how much this woman persisted that the breeder guaranteed her the puppy would stay at around the twelve inch mark at its tallest. Let's just say that with time, that dog turned out to be an amazingly friendly dog!!! But also a hell of a lot bigger than was ever expected.

Again, do your due diligence to find the right fit for your family!

Above : Gunner refusing to outgrow his puppy bed.
Below : Gunner proudly displaying his dog toy inventory.

13 ~ UNEMPLOYED DOGS

Apparently since 1999, the first Friday following Father's Day each year has been designated to "Take Your Dog to Work Day". Many prominent companies now actually have "Dog at the Workplace" company policies in order to accommodate employees taking their dogs to work. Why is that?

If you review the vast number of medical journals available, it becomes obvious that by and large, it's an accepted theory that pets, and dogs in particular are good for our health.

Dogs in the workplace are known to lower stress, and create comfortable, flexible environments for us. Further to that they are known to trigger interactions that may not have happened without them which in turn creates communication. With better communication this leads to more trust which is a key component for a successful work environment with less stress.

So I'm not a fancy schmancy statistician or analyst, but I know they've also done studies equating high stress and "sick" or "toxic" working environments to low employee attendance and thus high costs incurred to the company due to poor or low employee performance and attendance.

Gunner had quickly become a fixture at the environmental company that I was the financial controller of with his regular daily attendance. It's true what they say, it may be unconventional, but having dogs at the workplace truly does lift moral.

Since the day I had brought Gunner home, I had already planned out how I was going to "raise" this little guy to be the most well rounded, socialized, well behaved and obedient Doberman ever known to mankind. I was so eager and ready and with all my previous dogs, I had learned so much, I was quite confident that everything would be just perfect.

I want it understood that I did not buy Gunner with the immediate intent on having a show dog, I just wanted to have a real healthy relationship with my dog and most importantly, I wanted to have fun with my dog.

I'll be honest, I'd been single for quite some time and by "sometime", I mean years and now I felt like for the first time in my life, I was really living for me. The fact of the matter was that even though I prayed nightly to meet my soul mate, he never came along and I guess I just gave up. I don't think that's necessarily a bad thing, I think it would have been worse to get bitter or carry on miserably. But now with Gunner, I had focus, I had a new friend and I got really involved in the training and knowing this puppy.

When little Blaze came along, this I saw as simply doubling my fun! Even though Gunner was already a Canadian Champion and Blaze would likely prove to get her Canadian Championship as well, I didn't have any intentions of breeding and consistently stipulated that.

I always referred to the company I worked for as the "little company doing huge numbers". We had one inside sales person, a shipper/receiver, a purchaser and myself that worked full time during the week in the office. We had on average two to three outside sales representatives that we saw every so often and of course the two owners who we saw monthly, maybe a few times more then that. When I first started at the company, on occasion, we had people come in as walk in sales but for the most part, all sales came in via email or by phone.

Being the "working dog", I literally put Gunner to work right on his first day at the company. We followed a very strict routine not only for him but also because I am a very routine person and work better having somewhat of a "plan".

For our morning coffee/potty breaks, we not only went outside for the potty break but when we came in, we did basic obedience training in the warehouse.

This usually consisted of basic skills such as sit, stay, down, heel and then of course combinations thereof. For the record, it was strictly prohibited to teach this puppy "shake a paw" as I always thought for some reason that it was a stupid pet trick and therefore beneath him.

Gunner was an incredibly quick learner and proved that a little praise and food motivation would go an exceptionally long way. This break was only a fifteen minute break which seems short but for Gunner as a puppy, this was awesome as he had a pretty short attention span and did tire easily.

I will openly admit that on previous dogs, I had used "compulsion training" where a choke chain was the collar of choice. Where motivation was used for good behavior, "corrections" with the choke chain for bad behavior was used. With Gunner, I truly never needed to use a "correction" from a choke chain as a simple firm "No!" was more than enough to get the point across. In fact, I rarely even used the firm "No" as it usually shut him down into a complete "boo hoo hoo, woe is begotten me" state of mind where nothing could be learned. On the other hand, Gunner would do triple backflips for me with praise and a good pat!

Before Gunner came to work, at lunch time, everyone ate at their desks primarily or went out for lunch to pass the time. But with Gunner's arrival, everyone was now eager to eat in the lunch room which previously was never used for anything other than meetings.

During our half hour lunch breaks with the three other employees, we ate and "socialized" but also had "rules" for Gunner where he had both a little bed as well as a toy box in the lunch room. Coming in from potty break Gunner would go to his lunchroom bed and have his puppy snack and was required to stay on his bed until everyone was finished eating. I was never a fan of having dogs that mooched from the table, particularly large dogs so really wanted to insure that this was not allowed with Gunner. With Gunner's whole toxic gas situation, it was also very important to insure that he didn't eat table scraps.

During the first few days, Gunner came to the table immediately after finishing his lunch but I would just politely say "bedtime", I'd pick him up and place him back on his bed. Again, he was a quick learner and shortly he would eat and then lay down and wait.

At first he did his little puppy "woo hoo hoooo" cry, but even that stopped after a few days as we ignored him and he learned that it got him nowhere. I will say that hearing that little "woo hoo hoooo" cry did so tug at my heart and made ignoring him terribly difficult. It was all I could do not to go rescue that sorrow filled little guy!

After everyone finished eating, Gunner learned "break time" which meant he could now come off his bed and play if anyone wanted to. With him being so darned cute, particularly with his little fleece jacket on, everyone did want to play with little Gunner!

Our fifteen minute afternoon coffee/potty breaks were more of an adventure time where Gunner snooped around the 13,000 square foot warehouse with me following him to make sure he didn't get into too much trouble. This was for Gunner to venture out alone in the wildness of the great beyond, with me as back up in case he needed moral support.

Before long, we started hiding some of Gunner's favorite toys amongst the skids in the various rows of the warehouse for Gunner to "find" which made him even more eager to snoop things out. It's not until this very moment of my writing, that I do believe this is what lead Gunner to love his game with Tim of "Hide and Go Seek" so very much.

As time went by, Gunner so well adjusted to the "times" of the various breaks that he even told us when we were late for break. Heaven forbid that I be caught up doing something and ran a little past the schedule and Gunner would be right beside me at my desk poking at my arm with his nose. I'd glance at the clock and sure enough, we'd be running a few minutes behind. He had a built in alarm clock that was second to none!

Gunner was great in the office, with his schedule so set, he honestly slept for most of the day in his open door kennel until we had breaks. The only time he came out other than that, was when clients came in and this actually started happening a little more as people simply loved seeing this little Gunner grow up.

The "customer ritual" was always the same. The customer would come in, Gunner would wake up, take a few steps out of his kennel and do his classic "yawn, stretch, fart". All of us would turn green for a bit and everyone pretended it didn't happen. Truth be told to this day, I'm not sure who came up with "Sir Farts A Lot", whether it was me, one of my co-workers or even a customer. But everyone knew Gunner that way and everyone took it because it was Gunner's signature.

Sadly, our offices like most, did not have windows that opened so we simply had to wait for the air to clear. Again, there is no deodorizer in the world that would cover that stench up! It was terribly embarrassing but yet at the same time, it really helped start conversations on a funny note. Sort of! That's me being all "glass half full" like I typically am.

Being the financial controller, I was privy to all the financials of the company and was consistently looking for ways to grow the company, higher profits, cost effectiveness, more company recognition and overall increased productivity. The main problem that I saw with the company was that we had regulars who always purchased the same stuff. We had over 13,000 square feet of warehouse that with racking allowed for four rows upward of skids. Literally, we had thousands of products that no one knew about and how do you even begin to market that all at once?

I had worked previously at a marketing firm and so in putting two and two together, I started sending out marketing emails and brochures to our customers with "products of the month".

Gunner was not only our mascot but served in a lot of our advertising and marketing brochures and customers loved it! Heck they loved Gunner! Who didn't want to buy a high visibility shirt that looked so strapping on a Blue Doberman sitting on a skid of adsorbent material? In one photo shoot I had approximately a hundred different kinds of gloves all strewn in a pile and Gunner laid in the middle holding one in his mouth. Again, who wouldn't want one of those gloves?

I want to be crystal clear on all of Gunner's "work life". Gunner was amazing with the clients but that's also because he was always under complete control. I have always felt that no matter what anyone says, dogs are dogs and they can, under circumstances, bite even though you may think that they would never do such a thing.

This may sound like overkill but I've always treated large dogs like loaded weapons that if handled inappropriately, they can go off. Many people may read that and get upset with that statement but all I can say is that I've never had any of my dogs ever bite anyone. I'd rather be safe than sorry as in the end, it's the dog that pays the price if a bite occurs and typically, it's the owners fault.

I say Gunner was under control at all times, and he was. I had my own office which upon Gunner's arrival, immediately had a gate attached to lock him in my office but yet have the door open. When we went on breaks, Gunner was on leash and when we played with him in the warehouse off leash, we always insured that the company doors were locked so as no one could "sneak in on us". Customers would come in and come to my office door and if Gunner approached the gate, they were welcome to pat him over the gate but he was not ever allowed loose with them.

I did this purposely for the protection of Gunner so as he would always be able to "get away" if he didn't want to be with someone and it's almost as if he knew that. Another belief I've always had is to insure dogs always have an out. A way to get away from "danger" or a "threat" if they see or feel one. Given that allowance, a dog will typically remove itself from a bad situation before biting.

When customers came in, Gunner, for the most part would go say hello but on rare occasions he wouldn't, he would just stay in his kennel or "smile" from the floor of my office.

Oddly enough, we did have one customer that obviously had occasion to drink as he always reeked of booze. If Gunner was laying outside his kennel in my office when this customer came in, he'd actually get up and go into his kennel. It worked perfectly. He'd stay in there while the client was talking to our sales rep and only I could feel the vibration of the very faint growl that escaped from Gunner. I never did trust that guy and funny enough, neither did anyone else in the company.

So, Gunner was, I guess, not only the mascot and photo shoot model, but also the whole company's protection. I know for me, I always felt safe.

The problem with being hearing impaired is that you can't hear people coming so essentially, everyone is sneaking up on you which can be rather unsettling. Further to that, it was very common for me to have financials out on my desk which were of the strictest of confidential. When you combine the two, Gunner was perfect for helping me hear people coming and also keeping them out of my office.

The one thing I think I enjoyed most was seeing Gunner be such an amazing testament to the great nature of the Doberman breed! He was so polite and obedient and people consistently said they couldn't believe how nice Dobermans were and how wrong they were to think otherwise. This to me was awesome as I've always enjoyed seeing people who think one way learning something different.

I said before that Gunner brought up the company moral and it was definitely true! Where we were all cordial to one another, during stressful times, Gunner always seemed to lighten the mood.

For our inside sales rep, Gunner always seemed to break the ice between him and the clients particularly with his farting as it always started the conversation with our sale of the day being on gas masks. The other side was, I guess when there's nothing to say, you could always avoid the awkward silence with talking about Gunner!

About a year after Gunner started working with me at the company and just shortly after Blaze came and joined the pack, the economy took a turn for the worst. Fortunately, for me, I could see the writing on the walls in the financial statements and we did manage to hold on for quite some time. In the end I was forced to make the tough decision of who to let go in order to keep the company going during the hard time.

After great thought and discussions with the owners, we all agreed that I could train a bookkeeper to do basic entries and train the owners in analyzing the financials. My salary was the highest so given all the scenarios, it was the most cost effective decision to make.

After a few weeks of training the new bookkeeper, Gunner and I became officially unemployed.

The upside of this was that Gunner being the working dog that he was, decided that his best financial move would be to open his own dog toy company. I concurred!

In my mind, this would allow one of two things to happen. Either Gunner's dog toy company would take off and we could sustain ourselves on that or, it may help us through the dry economic time and maybe we could rejoin the company we'd left as we did so enjoy it there. Either way, I thought it would be a good way to ease Gunner out of his strict routine which he had now maintained for his young life.

The owners of the company allowed me to use a small section of their warehouse as well as their loading dock for shipping and receiving stock in trade for financial guidance.

Gunner and I now sold dog toys at the various dog shows by holding a booth which allowed for me to be able to afford entering Gunner and now Blaze in the shows which we so enjoyed. Also, I got to meet all the dog people and spend my full day "talking dog" which I really enjoyed! From a financial perspective, this was a solid gold decision as Gunner never destroyed toys but by this time, little Miss Blaze had proven her destructive qualities and shredded everything!

I like to think that we didn't sell just toys, I truly enjoyed talking to people about their dogs and really finding the most appropriate toy for their dog. I can't remember how many times I went to pet stores and the sales reps would swear up and down that this twenty five dollar miraculous toy was indestructible. I of course, would purchase them being the good mom I was but after getting it home, Blaze would have it gutted it in minutes.

My policy was tell the truth with my clients. If they asked me for a toy that was indestructible, I told them to go buy concrete or rubber farm tires and even then that wasn't a guarantee. But I did grade the toys I carried on the Gunner and Blaze scale which did at least give people more of a reality instead of false promises.

For the most part, I do believe it worked as I welcomed returns and very few came in. When returns did come back, nine times out of ten, they weren't even returns but exchanges due to lack of interest on the dogs part and I was fine with that as the last thing I wanted was an unhappy dog.

Because I took time to get to know people and their dogs, I really do believe I started relationships with those people. If there are any of you out there reading this book now, please know that I miss you and I'm very sincere when I say that I enjoyed talking to you!

My "Bull Terrier Ladies" were an amazing couple who showed a few different bull terriers. I could listen for hours to them telling me all the crazy things their dogs did and wonder to this day how they're doing. They had this precious little girl who I watched grow from a puppy into a wonderful show dog with all kinds of attitude!

My "Kerri Blue" people were another couple that I truly enjoyed. They had a girl that showed fabulously and the rule always was that the better she did in the ring the better the toy she got after the show. Gosh I enjoyed going ring side to watch and better yet when she came by the booth with her owners and picked out her own toy!

Another Bull Terrier couple had this big boy who was just a powerhouse and seemed so serious all the time but you could tell he had a heart of gold. One Christmas I had occasion to sell Christmas Green Velvet Bell collars that jingled when worn and the minute this big boy had one put on he just pranced! He trotted up and down the hallway jingling like a fool with this huge canine smile on his face.

I could go on for pages and pages with listing our clients and their dogs as we met so many amazing people/dog teams! I'll stop here though with one final mention as this "team" I became quite close to and miss to this day.

She is a wonderful woman named Joan, who with her husband owned and loved two show Pugs that did quite well in the ring. But Joan's heart was stolen by a larger than life rescue Pug/Japanese Chin cross named "Alfie" that she had adopted. Or maybe it's more appropriate to say that Alfie adopted her!

If I had to describe him, I'd say on the outside Alfie looked definitely more Pug than Japanese Chin but on the inside his personality was absolutely Chin! He was an intelligent little comedian with the heart of a lion! He always knew just exactly what toys he wanted and would never accept "no" for an answer!

Having said that, Alfie was always polite and always brought me his toys to be paid for as opposed to just "stealing" like most dogs. It's like he knew that Joan had to pay first!

I can remember the first time I experienced Alfie have Joan purchase a toy for him. He brought me the toy and then watched me as I figured out the sales taxes on my calculator! I swear to this day he knew the actual tax percentages the way he watched!

Because I was still showing Gunner during this time, as well as Blaze now, there would be occasions that I had to skip away from the booth and head to the ring myself. Gunner managed to persuade my Aunty Shirley to help out and she had as great a time as I did talking to all the people and meeting all the dogs. Before long, Aunty Shirley was also coming on the road with us to dog shows and working the booth.

Overall, Gunner's dog toy company worked out pretty good, we certainly weren't living large but we were living and I never was one for materialistic things. The big thing for me was, I was now home fulltime with all the pack unless I was going to the dog shows. But as much as I enjoyed the booth and all the dog and people teams we had opportunity to talk to, it was a pile of work loading and unloading all those toys.

On average, there was one dog show weekend a month so that left roughly three weeks of me on strict home time with the pack. This was great because with the Calder acreage, there was piles of grass to cut and over all yard work.

Though Gunner got a lot of socialization and obedience at the environmental company, he didn't get the physical exercise that I had hoped for. I had also thought that maybe the lack of physical exercise was possibly the contributing factor to his outburst with Vegas.

While working for the company, I also found that little Blaze wasn't getting near the attention that Gunner was. I really felt better with this as now I could dedicate more time to all the dogs.

It seemed to me that although Gunner and I were unemployed for the first time in our lives and I personally found this very scary, this could also prove to be the best time of our lives and particularly mine. Everyone would get the attention they needed as well as all the exercise and simply, I wouldn't be running around ragged like I had been for years just trying to survive.

Again, how quickly we learn!

Above : Gunner just before moving to Calder.
Below : Gunner at Calder

14 ~ AGGRESSION

Gosh I hate writing this chapter! I literally feel sick to my stomach in even starting it and don't know where to begin.

Gunner had the episode in late August of 2008 with Vegas which lead to the gaping head wound and all the stiches while I was still working for the environmental company. But it never happened again so it was seen by the breeder, myself and Gunner's vet as stress from moving into Calder and the change of routine.

That holy terror but much loved little Blaze joined the pack in that following late October or early November of 2008.

Manitoba is known for its long hot summers which reach well into the 30 degree Celsius range but yet we're also renowned for our cold long winters which can fall well into the -30 degree Celsius and last a long damn time.

The fall season of 2008 was a beautiful one and it seemed to go on, much to many Manitobans favor, forever. Call me crazy but I have always enjoyed raking my lawn and with Calder there was an endless supply of Oak and Poplar tree leaves of all different colours constantly littering the yard.

We spent our days now waking up, usually to Blazes "crack of dawn Jurassic park screech of the mighty

TRex". After the pack all devoured their breakfast like it was their last, we all headed directly outside for the day. It was very rare for us to spend any time at all in the house unless of course I needed a potty break. Typically, while I worked, the pack just played, snooped, hunted or in Blazes case, shredded expensive bushes I had planted.

If I had any running around to do, typically for groceries, Gunner usually joined me as the temperatures were right for him to wait in the Escape while I did my quick errands. Blaze was still too little and ill-behaved to be trusted in the truck so usually sat that out in her kennel with Vegas and Taxi.

I remember that fall morning being exceptionally beautiful. We had all had our breakfast, gone outside and done our normal routine where I spent a few hours raking leaves while the pack frolicked in the yard. I had planned that day, that after I came in for lunch, I'd shower and head into town to pick up my groceries for the next week.

I finished the raking, came in, had a quick bite, finished my shower, was dressed and in the bathroom putting my hair in my classic pony tail. As I stood in front of the sink starring into the mirror I felt the weirdest vibration in my feet and just an overwhelming ill feeling.

I stopped with the pony tail and with my arms still up, looked slowly to my left to see Gunner at the bathroom open door with this expression on his face that was not Gunner. His cropped ears were flat back against his head and his eyes didn't even seem to be the same colour as normal. He was growling at me!

In that split second that I looked at him, he jumped into the air at me now snarling and frothing at the mouth. All time stopped as we know it and went into an eerie soundless slow motion.

As he came at me in the air, my hands grabbed his throat and with the force of his body hitting me, I rolled to the side not letting go and the two of us fell into the tub. The shower curtain was ripped from the rod and now wrapped and tangled around us.

To this day I don't know how we got out of the tub but I remember me all of a sudden standing up and looking for Gunner and he was gone.

I didn't have a scratch on me, I hadn't been bitten, and didn't feel any pain which is surprising given the fall into the tub. But immediately panic set in as I now worried for Taxi, Blaze and Vegas.

I ran out of the bathroom screaming Gunner's name and the house was a flurry of dogs scattering. Blaze, Vegas and Taxi bolted from the living room and I ran past them to find Gunner there, on the couch and shaking.

He wasn't seizing, and he wasn't cold this time but he was terrified. His ears were still flat on his head, but his eyes were back to his normal colour and the most terrible whimpering was coming from him. In that moment, I'm not sure who was more terrified, him on the couch shaking and crying so bad or me standing and starring at the dog that just violently attacked me.

As I stood there staring, flashes of memories flickered through my head. I remembered that cute little puppy sleeping on my chest when we came home from work. The puppy breath. His little "woo hoo hoooo, woe is begotten me" cry. How he sniffed flowers and seemed to so appreciate the wonderful smell they gave off. All the smiles he gave to clients at work as he yawned, stretched and farted.

What the hell happened?

The only thing I knew right then was that he was terrified and literally didn't seem to know what had happened either. He didn't come to me, he was scared of me. You could tell he knew he'd done wrong but simply didn't understand why he had.

I've been attacked by dogs before while involved in rescue. I've had dogs corner me. I've seen their look when things go "south" and it wasn't the same look that Gunner had and they weren't sorry after because it was an attack they meant business with. Now I know maybe it sounds like I'm making excuses or trying to see things that weren't there, but Gunner and I had a bond. This was so not how we were together.

By this time, Taxi, Vegas and Blaze had run upstairs to the kennel room. I left Gunner on the couch and locked each of them in their respective kennels for safety and headed back downstairs to find Gunner still on the couch, still shaking but now throwing up.

I sat down on the loveseat opposite Gunner and called my vet to schedule an immediate emergency appointment. Fortunately, after hearing about the episode they told me to come in when I could and they'd make themselves and an operatory available. Now, I had to get Gunner to the truck.

Hanging up that phone set in a reality for me. I was alone, in the country with no neighbors close by to hear, and I had Gunner, an 89 pound male Doberman who just attacked me sitting within six feet of me.

I felt so terribly sore now from the tub fall. Every breath I drew caused sharp searing pains in my left ribs like I was being stabbed. My right knee was swelling and now I too was shaking along with Gunner. I'm not a doctor but maybe this was adrenalin I was now feeling? I wanted to throw up just like Gunner now.

It's funny during times like this the things we remember.

The next thing that flooded my mind was Ceaser Milan saying to be a "Calm pack leader". I watched his programs, not that I believed in the way he taught at times but I was always intrigued at how he seemed to not fear dogs no matter how they behaved. He did always seem calm even when dogs were attacking him. He never seemed to panic.

I stood up, passed Gunner calmly like nothing had happed and got his collar and leash. I returned to the living room and simply said in my happy voice "okay, car riding time".

Gunner looked at me, immediately stopped his shaking, his ears came up and he jumped off the couch and sat in front of me to accept his collar as was our routine. I put the collar on and we left the living room with him in heel position and headed to the truck. All his manners were back in tact!

As I drove to the vet clinic which was in Winnipeg, approximately a forty five minute drive away, Gunner laid in the back with his chest on the arm rest as per normal. For him, everything was literally back to normal. For me, tears were rolling down my cheeks as I remembered that lunging dog was now in the truck with me, driving down the highway with his face beside mine. Would he attack again? I could actually feel his breath on my neck when he turned his head to look out the window.

We made it to the vets' office and Gunner was tickled pink! He loved going to the vet! There seemed to be zero memory of what had occurred just an hour ago. In the parking lot, I called into reception and alerted them that I was there and they said they had an operatory ready for us and no one was in the waiting room.

I got out of the truck and being as calm as possible, I took Gunner's leash and said "lets go". Gunner jumped out of the truck, went into heel position and we proceeded directly into the vets' office and into the operatory.

Here I was again, the vet looking mortified, Gunner having a blast at the office, and me explaining how an unprovoked attack had happened.

You could tell the vet didn't believe me. Why would he? Gunner was doing great! He was in amazing physical condition, he was attentive and standing every so patiently expecting to be examined. His nubby tail wagged as he waited.

The vet did examine Gunner and completely without any fear at all. He took blood work, felt Gunner all over for any tender spots, examined his mouth and teeth, and listened to his heart. Standing back, and crossing his arms, he openly said that he couldn't find anything wrong. He had zero explanation for the behavior I described. Granted we'd wait for the blood work to come back but for all intents and purposes, there was nothing wrong with Gunner.

But I couldn't stop crying, I was scared. I was now scared of Gunner.

We left the vets office and headed home. As we turned left onto Calder, Gunner got up to look for the train that sometimes passed over the tracks we crossed. When no train was present, he moved to the left side of the Escape to look out the window for the cows he liked to see and bark at in the field that the farmer had.

We pulled into the driveway and he started getting excited as we were home now and he always loved coming home. I didn't love coming home today. I knew I had to get out of the truck but I had no idea what the hell I was going to do now.

I let Gunner out and once we got in the yard, I just left him outside while I headed in and went straight to the phone to call Mandy.

I was completely hysterical during that call when I explained again that Gunner had attacked and I had no idea why. It's weird, I felt like a fool. I knew so much about dogs and in fact, felt like I knew everything and in this case, I had no idea why it happened.

Mandy was amazingly calm. She had a lot of experience with not only having her own dogs and Dobermans in particular but from also working at the shelter in North Dakota.

Mandy asked so many questions and all I could keep saying was "I don't know, there was no reason".

Very firmly, Mandy said, "Karen, I believe you that you don't know, but there is always a reason, we just have to find out what it is."

We ended the phone call with the decision that we'd wait for the lab results to come back. There had to be some sort of medical reason. In the meantime, I had an obligation to the rest of the pack members to protect them so I'd have to keep Gunner separate from them at least until this resolved. Add to that, I needed to protect myself.

The thought kept ringing in my mind, what if I hadn't felt that vibration in my feet? What could have happened if he actually did get me? He was lunging at my face, my neck. This wasn't a dog who was taking an inappropriate nip at my leg or something. I could have been seriously hurt.

With all the dog showing I'd done at this point, I had ample dog kennels to assist in setting up zones. I placed a very large "homemade" kennel in the living room. I set up another three kennels in the dining room facing the living room.

From now on, I had to run two packs. Gunner was by himself with me, and Blaze, Taxi and Vegas would be together. At no time would Gunner be able to mingle with the others, or at least until we figured out what had happened.

The next few days I waited for the test results to come back from the lab and it seemed like years. The pack seemed somewhat okay but utterly confused as to why everyone was being shuffled all the time.

We would wake up and everyone would be fed, then Gunner went out to potty and came in to go directly into the living room kennel. I'd then let the others out to potty and come in to be loose for an hour. After that hour, they'd go potty and then come into the house and directly into the three kennels now in the dining room off the living room. Gunner would come out to potty and then have his loose time in the house which terrified me but I stayed "calm" and always kept my distance from him.

I was so thankful at this time that I had taught everyone the command "bedtime". And so thankful that everyone loved their kennels with of course the exception of Blaze. But even Blaze seemed to understand that this was the "new routine" now.

Three days later the call came in from the vet. I hate to say this but it was news I dreaded. Everything on the labs came back normal.

How can everything be normal? Everything about that attack was far from normal! And to say "normal" means that I can't fix this. As horrible as it sounded, I almost wanted to hear that he had a tumor or something. Give me something to hold on to for causing this. But there was nothing. Again I called Mandy.

To say Mandy was upset was an understatement. The one result we didn't have and didn't even test for was Hypothyroidism and that was her first question.

When I had taken Gunner into the vet, I had mentioned thyroid again but he again had dismissed it. Gunner was too young, he wasn't fat, he wasn't lazy, and he had a beautiful coat. Yes, he still farted a lot, still had loose poop, and of course the rashes due to allergies but that wasn't thyroid.

Mandy still pushed thyroid and I felt torn. She wasn't a vet and my vet was a long time experienced vet. He would know. Wouldn't he?

Either way, Mandy said my only options were to either live with running the two packs and over time reintroduce everyone or put Gunner down due to my fear of him. She didn't say that lightly either but she knew I was scared and she openly admitted she would have been scared too.

My dad is extremely stubborn and strong willed. It drives everyone in our family crazy how stubborn and strong willed he is. He has always told my sister and I that we can do anything. Anything we set our minds to. I take after my dad.

In my life, I've overcome a lot. This story isn't about me per se, but it's important for you to know what I'm about so as you can understand why I made the choices I did. I've survived a lot, I've worked hard, and I do believe I can do anything.

I left home when I was fifteen and moved in with my Gramma. When I continued to bounce around schools and not commit to my education, my Gramma gave me the choice of working at a job, joining the military or finishing school. I knew I wasn't very good at the school thing, so tried various jobs and always got fired within weeks. At seventeen, Gramma signed me over to the military.

I was one of three females to graduate from my basic training with honors. Instead of joining the military as a classic female trade such as cook or medic, I went in as a Weapons technician. This was back in the day when that wasn't very typical for a female. But I excelled.

Overall, I did my four year stint in the military and it gave me self-confidence and validated to me that I literally could do anything if I set my mind to it.

When I got out, I took a year course in Accounting and that's where I've stayed.

I progressed from being the receptionist at an Accounting firm to a bookkeeper and from there to Financial Controller. I don't have the alphabet behind my name because I don't have the education technically from books. Everything I have is real life experience and no one can teach that from a book.

At thirty years old or so while taking my hour and half bus ride to the dental office I worked at as their controller, I was engaged in a discussion with the bus driver. I remember it vividly as I needed to get my dad a father's day gift as well as birthday gift and had no idea what to get him. When I'd asked dad, he said he just wanted a t-shirt and I thought that was a terrible gift.

As the bus driver and I talked, he made a joke about me going into the Manitoba marathon because if I finished it, I'd get a t-shirt. He was joking of course because I was a smoker and had zero training in marathons.

This pissed me off to put it lightly. He was actually telling me I couldn't do it because I hadn't trained and I smoked.

When I got to the dental office, I stopped in at the jewelers down the hall that I always said "good morning" to and I told them that I was thinking about doing the marathon that was a few weeks away. They burst out laughing because again, I hadn't trained and I smoked.

Dad always said I could do anything.

I entered that marathon and I finished it without training. The moral support of my sister Sandy showing up at various locations throughout that marathon helped me push through the tremendous pain and I completed the full 26.2 miles.

I came in dead last, hallucinating that Jesus was beside me the last few miles and finished with a time of just over eight hours and got my t-shirt. When my dad saw me at the finish line and I gave it to him, he cried. I could barely walk for weeks after and couldn't do stairs for a few months. But I did it, because I believed in myself.

Why is this important? It's important because I knew I was facing a battle with Gunner. I could easily have put him down and I doubt anyone would have blamed me. But I couldn't in good conscience put him down without knowing the reason why. I believed I could take on this battle and find out.

I have said before, everything happens for a reason. I believe to this day that God gave me Gunner. He made him climb into my lap because He knew I'd fight for Gunner. I'd figure it out. And I would fight for Gunner.

And I did.

Above : Gunner and puppy Blaze getting along.
Below : Gunner, Blaze and Karen after a busy weekend
doing Rally at the Kenora Dog Shows.

15 ~ A TIRED DOG IS A GOOD DOG

The day I picked Gunner up at the breeders, I remember dad saying to me on the drive out that he thought I was making a terrible decision. My choice in the Doberman breed was a poor one because they were known to turn on their owners.

Now some two years later, Gunner had turned on me but I want to be crystal clear, I don't believe for a second, nor should you, that it was a "Doberman" thing. This wasn't a working dog thing, a large breed dog thing or even just a plain dog thing. This behavior is not normal but sadly has been recorded many times by any and all breeds big or small. The attacks that make the headlines of the paper are typically of large breed dogs because they cause the most damage.

I didn't know why he had attacked me but I sure as hell was going to find out as I owed it to him. Further to that, if I didn't find out the cause of the attack, then it would tear down everything I had learned about dogs. They are our companions. They are loyal creatures that specifically have been bred to be "man's best friend" and make great family pets. Mandy said, and I did believe that there always is a reason.

The next few months were rough around the house as it seemed like I was constantly running around and putting dogs in kennels. It was exhausting to say the least and very stressful!

Gunner hated being locked up while the others played and Blaze in particular hated being locked up while Gunner played.

I was nervous around Gunner and had to now create personal space barriers as I didn't trust him and still had fear. At the same time, the Calder house was so darned small, I had to also be always conscious of both Gunner and I having "escape routes" just in case.

My favorite times with Gunner was snuggling, he was such a good snuggler, if that's even a word. I had mentioned that Blaze wasn't a snuggler and I appreciated that, but I think I appreciated it because Gunner was my snuggler.

Now, I couldn't snuggle Gunner. What if he attacked? My only saving grace the last time is that when he attacked, there was distance between us. The distance gave me time to protect myself. Snuggling wouldn't give me any reaction time if he did attack so I had to stop. Being close enough to pet him also meant that I had no time to protect myself if he went "off".

The first while, my Aunty Dee checked up on me on a regular basis because she knew I was scared. Even with her fear of the situation, she still remained very supportive as she knew I had to try to figure things out.

It's funny, Aunty Dee always had small dogs and so I didn't think she'd "get it". I thought out of her fear for me that she would push me to euthanize Gunner but she was the opposite. She supported me whole heartedly in taking time to try and sort this problem all out. Her dogs to her are the same as my dogs are to me. They're family and she realized that this was something I just had to do.

My mother, who I didn't have the closest relationship with at the time, was also to my surprise, very supportive.

One day on the phone while talking to mom, she stated so calmly, "Kari, God gave you Gunner for a reason. He knew you'd be the only one to take Gunner on and He knows you'll do everything you can for him. He knows that if you have to stop it'll be the right time."

I believe to this day that seeing this side of mom helped me to try to better our relationship.

Dad had a lot of difficulties with Gunner and the situation at this time but never once did he ever say "I told you so" which I so greatly appreciated. Where dad was legitimately scared for me, he also never once told me to put Gunner down.

I read piles of books on dogs and every waking moment I had, I either watched dog training programs, or talked "dog" with people.

Again referring back to Ceaser Milan, "a tired dog is a happy dog". When Gunner was on "out time", I had him working. We were either playing fetch with my Cuz sling shot contraption, doing obedience drills, or he was following me while I cut grass on the tractor.

While working at the dental office years before, I had occasion to suffer from a number of migraines. When I had talked to one of the doctors about it he had said for me to keep a journal of sorts. He felt that a lot of times, things explained themselves through journals. Through that journal, I learned after a few months that the migraines always seemed to come after I drank a substantial amount of a certain type of frozen juice that I purchased from time to time. After I eliminated that juice from my diet, those migraines never happened again.

With Gunner, I had immediately started a journal from back when he was a puppy and had all the gas issues. But now I hit it hard with listing all our daily activities, what he ate and when, when and what his poop looked like and even down to his rashes.

I noticed that Gunner did have times where he got a "far away" look. I'm not sure how to explain what that looked like but he could be looking at me and it was as if he couldn't see me. It was almost a drugged, spaced out look of sorts. During these times I'd quickly say a command like sit or down and it seemed to snap him out of it.

He also had head tremors. Not many, but every so often his head would shake a bit. I noticed through the journal that this seemed to happen after he played vigorously with his toys. He had a large stuffed octopus that he like to shake the heck out of and did so every so often. The journal indicated that he had these head tremors after doing that.

Mandy had mentioned that she'd seen other Dobermans have head tremors from time to time and no one really seemed to know what caused them but they didn't seem to have any long term effects. She felt maybe it was more of a stress thing possibly or a muscle being over worked.

Just in case, I did get rid of the large octopus and while the head tremors seemed to dissipate, Gunner still did have them from time to time.

If he had these far-away look "spells" in the house on his out time, I'd quickly use the "bedtime" command and he'd head straight for his kennel. He'd lay down for a bit and the spells would go away. I'm not sure if it was the command snapping him out of it or maybe distracting him from it but it was a reassurance to me anyways. At least I was safe because he was in his kennel.

I was so blessed with the weather. For Manitoba, we had an exceptionally long fall that year and barely even had any snow for Christmas. But the long fall gave me opportunities to watch Gunner.

After a few weeks I had started to notice a pattern in Gunner's journal.

We'd typically eat first thing when they woke up and during his morning out time, we'd play Cuz slingshot for a long time to tire him out. A tired dog is a good dog! But I noticed after this is when he also seemed to get these far away looks.

I had read somewhere that weightlifters don't eat three meals a day but instead almost casually graze all day long as their metabolism is on high. Gunner, was to a degree, a weightlifter in the respects that I was running him hard during the days. Physically, you could see bulging muscles as he had an amazingly strong physique. At that time, I was only feeding the pack twice a day, once in the morning and then again once before bedtime.

After talking to the vet as well as Mandy, I decided and they concurred that this could be some kind of blood sugar thing. Maybe Gunner's metabolism was also on high and his gas tank was running out per se.

At that environmental company I worked at, the inside sales rep was diabetic and if he didn't eat by 11:30am, he became vile with his attitude and at times had even verbally abused people. We all learned quickly with him to shove a banana at him which he'd scarf down and make it through to lunch. This was because of his blood sugar level getting so low.

I decided that the pack would now be fed four small meals a day as opposed to the normal two. They got their first snack at wake up, another at noon, another at 5:00pm and last snack at bedtime.

The results were amazing! Not only on Gunner but the whole pack, well, with the exception of Taxi!

Blaze was still a growing puppy and she never went into a gangly puppy phase. She grew a lot better than Gunner did and sure maintained her weight better. Vegas seemed to not be as submissive as he normally would be. Taxi didn't have any changes but I thought that was because she supplemented her diet with rodents, birds and frogs.

But Gunner was amazing! He did a complete turnaround which excited me to no end.

He no longer had those far away looks and his gas even seemed to be better. He still had the gas but the farting wasn't constant. He also seemed to be more mentally "with it" or clear. His overall focus even seemed better. We could do obedience a lot longer before he lost interest.

After a few weeks of the new feeding routine, Mandy and I decided and the vet concurred that it was time to try to amalgamate Gunner back into the pack. I would maintain his physical regime of Cuz throwing as well as the feeding routine and see how things went.

The one thing I would say was that while he was still not allowed to sleep on the bed with me because I didn't completely trust him while I was sleeping, I did feel I could trust him a lot more now. He truly seemed miraculously happy!

The only negative changes I saw in Gunner was that he barked a lot in the truck at passing strange dogs. This behavior seemed pretty normal for an intact male dog though. He didn't go "crazy" at them but did show some aggression towards strange dogs. He showed nothing but excitement at the sight of Blaze, Taxi and Vegas and you could tell he wanted so badly to play with them again,

Slowly, I started giving Gunner out time with the pack and everything was back to normal!

Winter was upon us now and outside time was reduced terribly due to the cold but I had prepared for that. I felt that it was imperative to keep up the physical exercise for Gunner and with being limited to the house soon, I followed Ceaser Milan again and picked up a real cheap used treadmill.

During the winter months, Gunner jogged or brisk walked forty five minutes a day on the treadmill. After he was done, I put Blaze on the treadmill but only for a short time as she was still under a year old and I only let her walk on it.

I never had Blaze run on the treadmill as I had heard that while it can be great exercise, it can be very detrimental to run young dogs whose growth plates were still open. The rule of thumb I'd heard is wait until dogs, particularly large dogs, reached almost two years of age before running them hard.

Within another month or so, Gunner was completely loose both outside and inside the house with the pack and he did great.

Taxi and Vegas were up there in their ages so they spent most of their inside time snoozing on the couch. But Blaze and Gunner played together a lot and it was always appropriate play. After Gunner and Blaze tired themselves, Blaze would go lay down on the floor and Gunner would snuggle on the couch beside me as he always had.

Everything was right in the world again!

Until it wasn't.

I feel like such a fool typing this. Again, it was a normal day. We had made it through the winter, the sun was shining brilliantly and the pack had spent the early spring morning playing outside.

We came in for the pack to settle in for a quick snooze while I had lunch. True to form, Vegas and Taxi were on the couch, Gunner was beside me snoozing on the couch and Blaze was having a cat nap on the carpet by the love seat. I watched a little television while I ate.

After almost finishing my lunch, I felt Gunner's body beside me get "tight". At first I thought he was dreaming, maybe dreaming of playing outside or something. But before I knew it, he made himself big, started growling and jumped off the couch.

Before Blaze even woke up, he had her by the back of her neck and he was shaking her violently.

I threw my plate of half eaten plate of food and again like I had with the Vegas episode, I grabbed Gunner from the back of the neck.

Blaze was shrieking at this point and had peed everywhere. Taxi and Vegas were long gone from the living room and had actually sprinted into their kennels in the dining room.

Once Gunner let go of Blaze, she too sprinted to her kennel and I wrestled with Gunner trying to now bite me to get him into his kennel.

After I got Gunner's kennel door shut, I locked in Vegas and Taxi as well and pulled poor little Blaze out to check her over. She didn't have any broken skin thank God, but she was shaking terribly. This was one of the few times that Blaze snuggled me. She was really upset and I held her tight for quite some time. I think I did this not only for her but for me, trying to settle myself down.

I deemed Blaze to be okay physically and put her back into her kennel and made that again upsetting call to the vet.

After the call, I called Mandy again crying. This time, Mandy begged me to do a thyroid check and I vowed I would even though I didn't believe it was thyroid. At the very least, when the results came back, she would get off my back about it.

After I settled down, I again put on my very fake but convincing calm pack leader face and took Gunner to the vet.

Yet again in the vet clinic, I cried and explained yet another unprovoked attack by Gunner. Again the vet stood there shocked and in disbelief that this awesome spirited dog would ever do something like that and again Gunner stood there really excited to be at the vet. Same old, same old.

The vet checked every part of Gunner over again, took blood and this time I insisted on a separate draw of blood for a full panel thyroid check. I remember it clearly because my vet actually said, "If you want to go ahead and spend money on something you don't need, that's your business and I'll do it". And he did.

I want to talk about my vet here for a few minutes so as you understand our relationship. He was an awesome vet that I completely trusted with my dogs!

He was well experienced and was even the vet for my first dog, the Yellow Labrador, Rusty. I had known him for years as he had been the vet for all my dogs and even rescues I temporarily had. I recommended him to many people because he was a thinker. He commonly did things above and beyond what other vets would. And lastly, he really listened to me. He was big into trouble shooting and problem solving if that makes sense.

Either way, as awesome a vet as he was, he swore the thyroid test was a waste of money but did it anyway simply just to appease me. I explained that I believed him and I was only doing it to appease Mandy.

Whatever the results would be, we had very few options left explaining this unpredictable behavior and sadly, for our safety, Gunner was running out of options.

Four days later the results for Gunner's thyroid came back from the lab in Toronto, Ontario.

I was in the kitchen doing the dishes when the phone rang. I didn't have call display, so wiped off my hands, grabbed the phone and answered with a happy, "Hello?!?"

What came back was in a stern yet shocked voice, "I would have bet you everything I had and would have lost it all. Gunner's thyroid came back and he's dangerously low! We have to get him on meds right away. You need to come in and get the meds as soon as possible"

You could have knocked me over with a feather! The relief was absolutely amazing!

Finally, at just over two years of age, Gunner finally had a diagnosis of Hypothyroidism. He wasn't just "low thyroid" but he was dangerously low. Now I had something to work with!

The reading and research was to take a totally new direction!

Gunner at the time of diagnosis, not showing the "typical signs" of Hypothyroidism - a poor coat, laziness or a weight problem.

16 ~ MONEY, MONEY, MONEY

At roughly two years old, Gunner had finally been given a medical diagnosis of Hypothyroidism.

What is Hypothyroidism actually?

The thyroid gland is located in the front part of the neck. Its function is said to make a hormone called thyroxine that controls metabolism (the process of turning food into fuel). With hypothyroidism, the gland doesn't make enough of that hormone.

The more I read up on it, the more I realized that it actually was quite a common disease in dogs. Further to that, it not only effected Dobermans. Where various sites said that yes, Dobermans were a breed prone to it, it was also very common in Golden Retrievers, Irish Setters, Dachshunds, Boxers and Cocker Spaniels and a variety of other well-known breeds.

Most websites did say that it usually was found to effect middle-aged dogs (ages 4 to 10) of medium to large breeds. But many sites also stated a higher propensity of the disease to occur in neutered males and spayed females although vets were unsure why.

When I researched on the "why" or how it happens, many thought that in some cases of hypothyroidism, the dog's immune system actually attacked the thyroid. Other causes were listed as just the simple shrinking of the thyroid gland and, although rare, a tumor of the thyroid gland. After talking to many dog people, some also felt that possibly the hard playing of puppies or young dogs where they bit each other's necks in play may cause a trauma of sorts to the gland. No matter what the actual cause, most vets agreed on a basic list symptoms.

Today's date as I write this section is August 11, 2018, and for some giggles, I just now did a quick google search on Hypothyroidism in dogs. The "signs and symptoms" listed on many websites are: lethargy, generalized weakness, inactivity, mental dullness, unexplained weight gain, hair loss, and excessive hair shedding and poor hair growth.

Gunner had none of these symptoms which is why my vet probably fought against the test for so long. Truthfully, Gunner was exactly the opposite of every one of those recognized symptoms. None of these sites really said anything about aggression issues though or even mentioned some of the symptoms that he did have medically.

I kept reading and researching and refused to stop until I found out. Gunner obviously had thyroid issues but maybe he had additional behavioral issues not related to the thyroid. Maybe he had additional health issues that in conjunction to the thyroid was actually causing the aggression.

I spent hours sitting in front of the computer reading screen after screen. I talked constantly to people I thought could help spit ball ideas with me at dog shows. I even took Gunner to trainers for evaluations and special dog "behaviorists" and where some of them thought he gave "weird" looks, none of them ever saw any issues and couldn't explain anything.

Mandy advised me to a do some research in regards to a Vet in California, Dr. Jean Dodds, as she had some very interesting thoughts and findings in regards to Hypothyroidism as well as some additional signs and symptoms.

Quickly, I noticed that Dr. Dodds was very well accredited in her ongoing history of veterinary science. She even co-authored a book called "The Canine Thyroid Epidemic: Answers You Need For Your Dog" with Diana R. Laverdure.

Overall, Dr. Dodds has won multiple awards for her diligence and research. The more I read, it became obvious that this woman was not a "quack" although, she did outwardly speak against many common vet practices that I was so accustomed to, such as her difference of opinions of vaccine protocols and so forth.

As fast as I could, I purchased the book off the internet and sat down with a cup of coffee and literally read the whole book in one shot.

Please understand, I don't believe for a second that anything you read online should be taken as gold. But I do believe that when you find multiple sites, and multiple people making statements that supports a thought, even one not common, it's worth further investigation.

I won't go into extreme medical verbiage here or discuss Dr. Dodds book much further but I will say its one hell of an eye-opener and I highly recommend it for anyone who wants to gain more medical knowledge about their dog or canines in general.

What I will do though is say that when I read the almost two page listing of the signs and symptoms that Dr. Dodds mentioned in her book for hypothyroidism, I almost passed out.

Amongst the long list were: inability to fight infections, cold intolerance, mood swings, chronic infections, chronic offensive skin odor, greasy skin, skin infections, lack of libido, cardiomyopathy, diarrhea, and the list went on. Many of these mentioned symptoms Gunner did have and had been documented by me in his journal as well as his medical file

Further to that, the book stated that in early stages of hypothyroidism behaviors including lack of focus, aggression and/or passivity could present themselves. It also stated that dogs were now being diagnosed from the young age of ten months old and up. This was contrary to the belief that hypothyroidism only took place in middle age or older dogs.

Another draw from the book was a specific reference to a story about a dog named Tater and a situation he was involved in. I'll take a direct quote as it's terribly important here.

"Then, suddenly, Tater began to jump up without warning during sleep and roar like a lion. He attacked any person, animal, or thing nearby, and then would become fully awake, but unaware that anything had happened."

All I could think and still think today when I read that is, "Oh my god!" This was so Gunner and exactly what I had witnessed he'd done to little Blaze that day in the living room!

Gunner had gas, terrible gas and with it diarrhea or cow patty poop which on numerous occasions the vet had to actually prescribe the doggie version of Imodium.

I bathed Gunner twice a week because he always stank, had greasy skin and thought that would help the skin rashes and the "pimples" he got.

I always found it a blessing but yet odd that Gunner never tried to mount anything or mark territory other than the trees outside. Here he was this young intact male Doberman, and not once did he ever seem to display any sexual interest even at dog shows around females whom were in season.

And regarding the episodes of aggression, please remember that I said on numerous occasions that he'd have them and after they were done, he didn't seem to be even aware of what had happened. The episode where he attacked Blaze was almost verbatim of the Tater story in the book!

My last drawn direct quote from that book is this and please read it over and over again until it's completely imprinted in your brain:

"Sadly, millions of dogs are abandoned and/or euthanized each year for behavioral issues that could have been managed or reversed with the proper thyroid treatment."

As I read the book the first time, I only stopped at times to wipe the tears away and blow my nose. It was such a relief to read that so many of Gunner's problems were addressed here. At the same time, I cried because I hadn't taken Mandy's advice for so long to test for thyroid issues. Where it was a relief to finally have a diagnosis, I felt so terribly guilty that I hadn't found it sooner.

The good news was that I had found the "reason". I'm not a vet, but I do firmly believe even to this day that if I had tested Gunner back at five months, I think he would have shown then to have thyroid issues. But focusing now on the positive, the treatment was easy. Two cheap pills a day!

For the next few months, Gunner and I took trips to the vet on regular occasions. With the hypothyroidism diagnosis we knew he had to be on pills but at the same time it was very important to make sure that the right dosage was given.

The rule of thumb that the vet and I followed was to up the dosage, wait a few weeks while watching Gunner's behavior and then re-draw the blood and send away again for analysis to watch his levels. Both the vet and I thought we we're doing pretty well at this but sadly, it wasn't as easy as it seemed and we did make a terrible error.

The whole point of the medication is like any medication, it has to be properly absorbed into the system in order for it to work and this proved from time to time to be difficult but only after the fact did the vet and I realize this.

As we continued to test Gunner, his levels originally climbed to the "normal" function mark but then started to drop again. Under advisement of the vet, we agreed to continue to increase the dosage but again, Gunner's levels dropped, which simply made no sense.

With the levels dropping, Gunner's aggression seemed to increase and he had multiple outbursts directed at the dogs. Fortunately because of keeping Gunner physically apart from the other dogs, they were never hurt. But his lunging at the kennel at them or the intense growling outbursts did prove to traumatize them. You could see that on many occasions, Blaze, Taxi and Vegas were nervous of even passing Gunner's kennel.

Due to the last episode with Blaze, I had decided to keep Gunner segregated from the rest of the pack until I was positive that he'd never have these episodes again. That time never came and now I was almost more frustrated, as where I thought we'd found the solution in the treatment of his hypothyroidism, we seemed to be going backwards as now Gunner's outburst were even more frequent.

I will openly admit, I was emotionally exhausted at this point. Where I had endured and finally felt the relief of the diagnosis, things were getting worse by the day. I cried a lot and I lived in fear again. But I cried because seeing Gunner like this broke my heart, he wasn't happy.

My last ditch effort was a direct phone call to Dr. Dodds and amazingly enough, she took my call.

I explained all of Gunner, the symptoms, the episodes and yes that he was diagnosed finally with Hypothyroidism. I explained that he was on thyroid meds but where he originally seemed to be getting better, he'd now after months, gone down the toilet and seemed to be even more aggressive than before.

I remember Dr. Dodds asking me how much the dosage was for Gunner and when I stated the amount, she was mortified. She openly stated that he was over dosing on the level he was currently on and that he needed to be immediately removed from all meds until his system cleaned out and then started back on his meds. She recommended a minimum and maximum amount that he should be on and also warned me that during this time I needed to be particularly careful of his aggression possibilities. Further to that, she openly stated that all of his hair could fall out during this time of being med free.

This was relief for me but at the same time, I felt more sadness as I also felt I had failed Gunner yet again.

As the vet and I talked, we tried to figure out how we had been so diligent yet so wrong.

I refer back to where I mentioned the importance of proper absorption of meds into the system. Looking back in the journal I kept for Gunner and his medical files, we had noticed that where his diarrhea had cleared up upon first going on the thyroid meds, during two of his blood draws, he was suffering from diarrhea. This meant, that during those blood draws, he wasn't absorbing the meds properly so therefore, we had false reads of his thyroid levels falling.

As we continued to up the dosage, his diarrhea increased and therefore his absorption fell even more. We had a snow ball effect going on here that we didn't notice. This led to Gunner being overdosed.

I spent three weeks watching my every move with Gunner while he was totally off all meds.

After the three weeks were up, we tested Gunner again, placed him back on the prescribed amount from Dr. Dodds and in no time, I had my Gunner back! We confirmed this by again retesting Gunner after a few weeks and then every month thereafter for about a year and his levels stayed consistent.

I've always believed in vets and following through with yearly exams, heart worm and Lyme prevention as well as shots. But after all was said and done with Gunner, I estimate the total financial costs on vet visits alone ranged close to the $10,000.00 mark in his first three years if life. This of course takes into consideration all the vet visits for diarrhea, skin rashes, behavior issues, sugar level testing etc. I have never in my life experienced vet bills of that amount on a dog but will say that where it put me into a dire financial position, I never regretted it.

I needed to not only find out for Gunner what was going on, but for myself. I needed to know I was doing everything in my power and I did.

Do I recommend that anyone else ever do this? I'm not sure how to answer that. I think truly only you can answer that for yourself.

I've often said to friends and family that if I was married and had children, Gunner would have been put down at the first aggressive situation as I wouldn't be willing to take a chance with other people's lives. But that's me.

I said numerous times to myself that when I got Gunner, I knew everything and I truly believed I did. I was so arrogant! This whole situation was such an eye-opener moment that no matter how much you know, there is even more you don't know. To say it was humbling is an understatement.

I was single while this was going on. I physically protected the other dogs from Gunner and so I was really the only one that was ever in jeopardy while I was trying to figure it all out. I will say though, where the other dogs were safe from physical harm, they did suffer mentally and for that I'll always feel terrible.

When Blaze had arrived, she proved to be such a little fire cracker of a puppy! She was incredibly outgoing, energetic, and always bounding around and checking things out. With what seemed to be a constant wagging nub of a tail, she feared absolutely nothing. Now at just shy of a year old, she had turned from that happy fire cracker to what was quite timid and insecure and this was in great part to the terrifying interactions she had with Gunner. Blaze simply didn't feel safe in our home.

Vegas was a complete basket case at this point.

As I had mentioned Vegas had been found by Isaac back when I lived on Furby Street and had been extremely abused. He had remained submissive and nervous all his life but particularly had a tough time when Isaac passed away.

I remember as Isaac got older how I mentioned to Aunty Dee that I was considering putting Vegas down with Isaac because I didn't know how he'd make it without him. Vegas relied on Isaac for his wellbeing and went to Isaac for comfort from all his fears.

When the day came for me to take Isaac in for his last vet visit, Vegas was still in exceptional health even though he was considered by this time a "senior". I remember thinking that there was no way I could put Vegas down, but I so worried at how he'd move forward. I'm sure as you read this you're thinking I'm half crazy for even suggesting it but Vegas was completely dependent on Isaac for everything. Isaac made Vegas whole and that's why I often said at that time that I had one dog and Isaac had his dog.

When Gunner joined us, I saw such a rejuvenation in Vegas. Where Vegas was still incredibly timid and nervous, Gunner was a great distraction to Vegas from all of his fears. That was until Gunner became one of Vegas' fears.

At this point, virtually everything terrified Vegas and he had no distractions from it. On numerous occasions, I came home from work to find blood in his kennel because something had scared him. He'd actually break his teeth off at the gum line in trying to chew his way out through the metal cage. But if he wasn't in his kennel, he was even worse!

After multiple vet visits with Vegas now, I had tried aroma therapies, thunder shirts, leaving radios and the television on to drown out sounds, everything under the sun to try to settle him down. He'd have his good days and then something would set him off like a thunder storm and it would take days of him panting, pacing, crying and being downright terrified before he'd come back from it.

I was so terribly torn! In my mind all of this was my fault. If I had worked harder and faster to find the root of Gunner's problems then none of it would be like this. I couldn't put Gunner down because that was my fault. I couldn't put Vegas down because things were going to change soon. I felt like I'd ruined Blaze and contributed to her spirit being broken.

Taxi was the only one who didn't seem to give a rip about any of this or any of the drama in the house. As long as she could hunt, she was fine! If Gunner growled at her through the kennel, she snapped right back at him.

I though, was miserable. What had I done and what was I going to do next.

How long could this go on and how much more damage would I allow to the other dogs in this house and myself?

Above : Puppy Gunner
Below : Gunner at Calder

17 ~ MICHELE AND THE LIST

A reason, a season or a lifetime. I had never heard that expression until I met Tim but I do now believe that it's true. That's why people come into our lives.

When I first started showing Gunner, I was soon invited to join the local Doberman Club and did so. It was here during my first meeting of the club that I attended where I met not only fellow Doberman lovers but in particular a very important woman by the name of Michele.

Michele was a bit older than myself and quite small in stature. Where I was 6'0" tall and probably weighed in at 180lbs, Michele was quite the opposite and probably was lucky to touch 5'5" and quite tiny size wise.

As we sat outside for the meeting in the grass, Michele and I just started chatting and before you knew it, we were laughing. I'm not sure what it is with some people but sometimes you just connect and we did.

Michele wasn't currently showing Dobermans anymore but had for many years both bred and showed Dobermans with her spouse who had passed away a few years earlier. At the present time, she still had two of her Dobermans and was still very fond of the breed.

As we talked, we were quite surprised to find out that even though we both lived out in the country, we were actually only about a five minute drive from each other.

This five minutes would become very important to me and especially Gunner!

For this tiny woman, I was shocked at how much heart, kindness, compassion and knowledge she could pack into her little frame. She carried herself with confidence and was truly someone whom I quickly learned to respect. She was a wealth of knowledge about the Doberman breed and had so many stories that she was more than willing to share with me and I enjoyed listening!

Michele, like Mandy, quickly became another "go to" resource for me about Gunner and his issues and she again like Mandy, always answered her phone. But to take it one step further, Michele was always willing to drop everything and come over in a heartbeat if an emergency situation came up and did so on many occasions.

Upon Gunner meeting Michele when he was around seven months old, he too quickly became attached to her which wasn't surprising to me at all. You couldn't help but feel a strong "kindness" from Michele. Humans felt it immediately as did animals, a kindness and a sense of calm all from this tiny lady who had such a big personality.

Our relationship grew to where I have no question in my mind that not only did I consider her a friend but also a very trusted and strong support system for me with Gunner.

She was completely aware of all the problems that Gunner had and without judgment, she consistently offered sound advice but she also said she didn't feel he was normal. He wasn't a normal Doberman. She didn't mean this in a hurtful way as she had grown to also be very fond of Gunner but she had concerns for he and I. In Michele's experience, there was something wrong with Gunner, but what?

At one point when Michele felt like I still needed more information and troubleshooting she informed me about email "groups" or "lists" online that may be of further assistance with Gunner.

She had stated that you could sign up to be part of the group and you could email questions or concerns which would be posted publicly to all group members as would any of their related replies.

I quickly found three online support groups, one which was my local Manitoba dog group for all types of dog lovers. The second was a US based Blue Doberman group which had of course people with all colors of Dobermans but specialized primarily in the dilutes. From that group, I was informed of the US based Rescue Doberman group which seemed to also delve in conversation into behavior problems. The two Doberman groups in particular held a wealth of knowledge for me and many of the people offered not only personal opinions but there were also vets in those groups who would offer medical opinions.

I quickly began posting my problems online and in true form these groups were so helpful! Together, Mandy, Michele and these groups were all the support I could ever hope for. Where I was alone, I was so blessed to have so much help!

When Gunner had started to show signs of aggression, Michele too was mortified and in disbelief but she kept her head calm at all times as we talked about the situations. When she would come over afterwards, this tiny lady never showed fear towards him which amazed me because I had begun to fear Gunner and his unpredictability.

During the three week dangerous period when Gunner had been taken off all thyroid medications, it was Michele that got us through and helped me keep my emotions level. As Dr. Dodds had warned me, during this time of weaning Gunner off of all the thyroid meds so we could re-establish the correct dosage had made him very unpredictable and quite aggressive.

I remember waking up the one fateful morning with so much hope, we only had a few days left until Gunner would be back on his meds, we were so close! But as I rolled over in bed to look at Gunner in his closed kennel, he was already awake, staring at me and growling. Quickly my heart sank.

Leaving Gunner in his kennel, I quickly fed and pottied Blaze, Taxi and Vegas and called Michele.

"Hey Karen, what's up?" she asked.

With tears streaming down my cheeks and a shaky voice, I muttered out, "I can't do it anymore Michele, I have to put him down. I'm so sorry but I'm terrified of him!"

"Call the vet and see if they can get you in, I'll be over in five minutes!" she calmly stated.

It seemed like forever to me, but Michele did arrive in probably just the five minutes and came upstairs right into the bedroom to check on Gunner. As she approached the kennel, Gunner still laid there growling.

"Hey Buddy, what's going on? Not feeling so good are you Gunner?" She asked him and turned to me. "Where's his muzzle Karen? You're right, he's not right. Look in his eyes, those aren't Gunner's eyes. We'll get him into the vet and you can decide what you need to when we get there. For now, let's not worry about that, let's just go and see what the vet can offer. We'll take it one step at a time and it'll be okay."

It may seem odd, but while waiting for Michele, and through my tears, I had posted the morning's situation with Gunner to the Rescue Doberman group and informed them that I thought I was taking Gunner in to be put down.

While Michele in her short stature, got Gunner's muzzle on, the emails started coming into my blackberry.

The emails were panicked and it was obvious that the people responding didn't feel they had much time but wanted to email shows of support to me. They were kind and offered words of understanding and prayers.

The forty-five minute drive to the vets was a rather quiet one as simply no words could be found by either Michele or I. This had been going on for so long now. Gunner obviously seemed to be suffering, the rest of the pack was suffering and I was terrified of Gunner.

As we drove, I remembered the so many happy times with Gunner. All my aunts and I snuggling on the floor with all the puppies the day Gunner picked me. Gunner farting his whole way home the first day. Gunner riding on the forklift at work and the lawn tractor at home. The snuggles, the dog shows, our times in the Rally ring were proving to be so much fun and we were becoming such a great team!

How does this happen? That first car ride home had so much promise for me. I had started with such a dream of happiness and future and this is where it ends up? Having a two year old beautiful dog, your best friend, wearing a muzzle in the back of your Escape as you drive to the vets to put him down? Why? I was a good person… Why?

We arrived at the vet clinic, I pulled into the parking lot and turned off the truck.

Michele spoke quietly, "Karen, you have been through more than most others would ever tolerate. You have tried so hard and Gunner knows that. You have a decision to make that I will totally support and completely understand. But ask yourself the question before you go in there, do you feel in your heart you've done everything you can? I say this to you knowing you and knowing your relationship with Gunner. Whatever you choose to do, you have to have a clean heart or it will eat away at you for the rest of your life."

At that exact moment, Gunner from the back of the Escape slowly came up to us, laid down so carefully, whined softly with his muzzle on and tried to give me his paw.

I walked Gunner into the vets' office and up to the counter. My eyes were swollen from all the crying and my shirt wet from the tears that kept coming and wouldn't stop.

The kennel tech came out and took Gunner's leash from my hands and as she started to walk away she asked, "Do you want us to proceed with what you've scheduled?"

Gunner looked at me again with those eyes I now knew, and in a whisper I replied, "No, please don't put him down. Just neuter him. I'm sorry to screw up your day but don't put him down, I need him away from me for a bit. Please neuter him. And please have the vet call me."

I went back to the truck, got in, and broke down like I had that day when I had to put my Isaac down. Michele didn't say a word, she just put her hand on my shoulder and waited for me to finish having my moment.

When I had collected myself, I explained. "Michele, I couldn't do it! I love him too much. Maybe if he's drugged up for a few days, I can take it until we get him back on the proper amount of meds! I have to figure this out!"

With understanding and a strong grab of my hand, she stated with a shaky voice, "Karen, when he came up to us in the truck and whimpered, he knew why you brought him here today. I didn't think it possible, but he knew and he isn't ready either. I think you're right, for now, let's try this. Maybe it'll give us time to figure it out."

We drove home and spoke of how to get Gunner and I through the next few days. If I could only hold on for a little bit longer!

A few hours later, the vet did call to let me know that he understood both of my decisions. The neutering had gone well and Gunner was in recovery. The vet stated that if I wanted, I could pick him up that evening or give myself a break and pick him up in the next few days.

I went back the next day and got Gunner, he was so happy to see me and I him, but I still had my fears. I'd had twenty four hours without Gunner though, time to relax and think. I now had a little bit of new found strength.

I had notified everyone in the email group of my change of heart and they all had quickly replied again with support and prayers.

When I picked Gunner up, the vet handed me two bottles of pills and said, "I wouldn't normally do this but given the circumstances regarding Gunner and the history, the first bottle is his new prescription of thyroid pills and the second bottle is of heavy tranquilizers. As you know, we still have a bit of time that'll take to get him leveled off with his thyroid. If you have a problem with him again, if you were to give him a high volume of the second pills, they will cause him to fall asleep quickly and he will pass away."

I understood completely.

The next morning, Gunner received his first dosage of .7 of Thyrotab for his Hypothyroidism with his breakfast and he was to receive another .7 at his bed time meal. Ideally, the doses of thyroid meds are done twelve hours apart. It had been said that typically .1 should be dosed for every ten pounds a dog weighs and Gunner had weighed in at 89lbs at his neutering. We purposely started a little low with the intent of doing yet another blood draw in a few weeks.

The neutering did slow Gunner down for the next few days and kept him very quiet. He didn't mind at all the fact that he was mostly kenneled for those few days which did give me the reprieve I needed.

Both Mandy and Michele checked in on me regularly during these days to see how we were all doing. I had noticed almost immediately with the thyroid pills that Gunner seemed so much clearer! So far so good!

I have mentioned that during the day that I took Gunner in to be neutered, I had received so many emails of support and prayers from my email groups. But I had also received one email that was quite scathing and mean. The email had said how stupid I was that it had taken me so long to put him down. The email author said she was happy that he was finally dead. It was a cruel and angry email that I really held on to for a long time. I still have it to this day in fact, with all the others. This email though, gave me strength!

I think the email was similar to those people who said I couldn't do the marathon. Those people, as they laughed at the idea of me doing 26.2 miles without training fueled me, and drove my every next step I took on that marathon. I did finish that marathon, albeit dead last but I did finish.

That mean and nasty email, made me fight even more for Gunner and it paid off!

Within a week of Gunner being back on his meds, I noticed the changes in him. He showed more happiness and seemed to be much more in control of himself. He wasn't overly active due to the soreness from the neutering but he did seem to be getting along quite nicely! There wasn't any growls coming from him or quick aggressive lunges. This was all incredibly positive!

After three weeks had passed, we drew more blood from Gunner and retested his thyroid. His numbers had come up to the bottom of the "Normal range" but the vet and I still wanted them up just a little bit higher so he was prescribed with .8 Thyrotab twice a day.

Another three weeks after that Gunner was scheduled for yet another retest of his Thyroid levels. The day before this retest though, something had turned his belly and his diarrhea had started to flare up. This time, I knew better, I got him on his diarrhea pills, and postponed the blood draw for a few days later. At that blood draw, the results came back excellent! His numbers were almost bang on mid-range for "Normal" and the proof was in the pudding, Gunner was happy as a Lark!

For the rest of Gunner's life, he stayed on .8 Thyrotab twice a day and was an amazing dog!

Having said that, I had to be careful as when Gunner got his bouts of diarrhea which were a lot fewer and far between, this did effect his thyroid pill absorption rate which in turn affected his mood. He was never allowed to run loose with the pack again, because simply I still had concerns in trusting him but he never did aggressively lunge at any of them or me again.

It became quite the habit, really, if he for whatever reason threw up, I spent the next day on "alert" for his mood. If he got the runs, again, the next day I was on "alert". I learned to know Gunner probably more than most people know their dogs in the respects that I learned that his eyes told me when he was "crabby" which was very rare now but still did happen.

I kept in contact with the email lists and became quite the advocate for thyroid testing and still recommend it regularly to people I speak to now. People knowing Gunner's story started contacting me for help and I'd offer my historical advice. In many cases, when people were given the diagnosis of allergies for example, they tested for thyroid and were surprised that it was in fact thyroid problems.

The same was true with a variety of other ailments as well as behavioral problems. Once the owners pushed their vets to test for thyroid and the dogs were treated appropriately with thyroid supplementation, a lot of the issues resolved themselves.

As Dr. Dodds book stated, Hypothyroidism wasn't just a Doberman thing by any means. Over the years, I talked to Golden Retriever people, Siberian Husky people, Malinois, cross breeds, rescue dogs, breeds of all types, and dogs of all sizes and ages. Hypothyroidism is truly an epidemic in the Canine world! It can cause so many different problems and yet it's missed regularly by the trained professionals we so trust. I believe this is so commonly missed because many vets or owners have the tunnel vision thought that hypothyroidism symptoms are limited to weight gain, lethargy and poor coats.

People often asked me why I didn't neuter Gunner sooner as many have thought that it should have been obvious that the aggression was due to the testosterone. As much research as I did, there were just as many vets pro neuter or spay as there were vets against it. Many vets who knew more about the thyroid issues felt that neutering or spaying actually worsened the problem.

I never kept Gunner intact so as to breed him. I knew I'd never breed him particularly when he seemed to have so many health issues. But it was also my belief that spaying or neutering shouldn't be done until the male or female dog had physically matured. I'm not a vet, never have claimed to be a vet and never will but I always likened early spay or neutering to performing hysterectomies on pre-teen human girls. In that case scenario, I think it would do extreme harm to a young girl in her most complex growth stage. What does this early spaying or neutering do hormonally to the body and how does it affect our canines' growth?

I guess at the end of the day, it's everyone's choice of when they spay or neuter. I know I don't believe in indiscriminate breeding of dogs and obviously early spay or neuter prevents that. I've had intact males and females in my home at the same time and never had any situations that resulted in an unexpected litter of puppies. To me, it's a matter of being a responsible owner.

If you're on the fence about spaying or neutering, I recommend to you as I always have, do your due diligence! Read up, educate yourself, speak to your vet and come to a meeting of the mind and do what works for you, your family and your pet!

Back to the mean email that I received about taking Gunner in to put him down. I never addressed it in the email group publically but about a year later, the woman emailed me again.

She told me her story which was identical to Gunner's. She had a male Doberman who she adored but never was diagnosed with hypothyroidism and as much as she loved him, with his aggression, she had made the decision to put him down. She admitted she was angry at me. She was angry that I was trying so hard and she was feeling like she had failed her boy for not trying as hard.

Sadly, over the years, I received a number of emails from people who took comfort in Gunner's story because they too had put down their beloved pet because he or she out of the blue attacked them. Where it broke their hearts to put them down, they now seemed to have a resolve of sorts that it wasn't anything they did, but possibly a disease that hadn't been properly diagnosed. Granted yes, they could have treated it and easily, but many didn't know. Many still don't know!

That is why I write this book! In the hopes that someone, even one person will be triggered to test for Hypothyroidism. That maybe a vet might have a dog come into his or her clinic with some weird symptoms besides laziness, poor coat and overweight and test for thyroid anyways.

The whole point of this book is to share what I've learned. To share where I failed so others might not, and to share where I've succeeded so others might succeed faster!

Above : Little Liar at five weeks old, still with Mandy.
Below : Blaze and Liar relaxing at Calder.

18 ~ LIAR, LIAR, PANTS ON FIRE

From the time of Gunner's neutering in late 2009, until May of 2012, our life was somewhat of a happy blur. As I look back, it's the fond memories I have that I keep in my heart.

Gunner stabilized on his thyroid meds and we spent a lot our time showing now in the Rally ring where the two of us had a lot of fun, some embarrassments but many laughs! We did have occasions to enter back into the Conformation Ring as well as the CKC started allowing the showing of Altered Dogs.

During this time, little Ms. Blaze also quickly achieved her Canadian Championship in the Conformation ring but didn't seem to enjoy it quite like Gunner. She more simply put up with it and humored me. Once she got her championship, for the most part, she was pulled from that due to her lack of enthusiasm. I tried her also in the Rally ring and where she did pass, again she never really enjoyed this either so it, as well was short lived. The whole point of me showing the dogs was it gave us something we could enjoy together, I definitely didn't want to force Blaze into something she had no interest in.

Gunner did have his dog toys that we were selling at booths at the shows so the three of us would pack up for the weekend, go to the shows and have a blast. I'd bounce from the dog toy booth with Aunty Shirley and Blaze keeping an eye on that and into the ring with Gunner.

Gunner still had the occasional issues but this was now a lot more predictable as it was solely based on his thyroid medication absorption level. Sometimes I would have to pull Gunner from a day of shows just because I knew he wasn't in the mood for it and may be a little "dicey" with his behavior.

The Rally ring became Gunner's favorite place and my preparation for him going in was always the same. I'd squat down in front of his kennel outside the show ring and say ever so nonchalant, "Gunner? If I was dog, I'd want to do the Rally." At this point I would get one of two reactions.

If Gunner would sigh deeply showing he wasn't particularly interested, this would be my cue to dodge the bullet and I'd pull him from that show. If Gunner jumped up in his kennel with a smile on his face, wagging his whole bum and little nub and he gave me those squinty eyes, it meant it was on!

It was if in that moment he was saying to me, "Mom! I'm a dog, and yes! I'd LOVE to do the Rally!" My reply was always, "You're right! You ARE a dog! Let's go do the Rally right now!" And off we'd go with him hopping happily beside me.

I say that Gunner would have a smile on his face and I know there are people out there who don't believe it but he did smile! The sides of his mouth would angle up so high on his muzzle that he actually got what I called "squinty eyes". The happier he was, the more squintier his eyes got to the point where you knew he couldn't even see out anymore.

As we'd walk towards the show ring, Gunner would look amongst the crowds of people looking for "his" people.

There was Aunty Cindy who was a professional handler who also bred Dobermans from time to time. On a few occasions when I was showing both Gunner and Blaze, she had helped me out by showing Gunner. She knew his history and accepted him for who he was.

Gunner adored her and when he'd spot her in the crowd, it was hard at times for me to hold him back. Aunty Cindy would take one look at him and open her arms up, and with that, Gunner and I would approach quickly and he'd jump right up and give her a smooch right across her face!

Jim was another professional handler who Gunner took to and had on a few occasions also helped with taking Gunner in the ring. Ed was the husband of Gunner's breeder and showed Gunner when he was just a young pup. Ed's breed of choice was Rottweilers but while they raised the litter of Dobermans in their house, Ed said that Gunner had stolen a piece of his heart and you could tell that Gunner always remembered him.

Aunty Carol also played a very important role in our lives. I talked at great lengths to her about Gunner as she had originated in showing Dobermans and moved into Rottweilers as her breed of choice. There were many times where she took Gunner into the ring for me as I wasn't emotionally prepared but yet he was. Carol knew him and Gunner adored her as well.

Chrissy was a wonderful woman who also had the Rottweilers as her breed of choice but she helped us out in the Rally ring. She, with a lady named Donna taught Gunner and I the various rules and helped us learn the fine art of Rally.

Aunty Tracy was another favorite of Gunner's. I don't think she ever took him in the ring but she was always present ring side as she showed Dobermans as well.

For whatever reason, one day Gunner just smiled at her and from that day forward she always called him "Gunnerroo". Tracy and I actually became friends because of the relationship Gunner had started.

All of these people and more knew Gunner's bad side but accepted him as he was because they also saw so many of those squinty eyed smiles and they adored Gunner!

Our home life was back to routine with the pack now that Gunner was stable. It was difficult in the beginning because Gunner could never be allowed to play with Vegas, Blaze or Taxi, but I learned to make accommodations.

I had the various kennels around the house to keep them separate and for the outside play, Dad had help me put up another fence in the large three acre play area so that all of us could be out together.

My cousin Johnny, being an amazing welder, helped me modify the back end of the Escape by welding a special barrier so that all dogs could be in the truck for car riding yet they were all kept separate from Gunner.

I'm not going to lie, it was a pain in the behind for sure but we all got used to it and finally lived harmoniously for quite some time!

Sadly, Vegas passed away in the winter of 2011 due to his old age and again, I felt that hole in my heart. Where the pack and I carried on, he was a real tough loss for Blaze as they spent a lot of time playing together.

Taxi was older than Vegas but she was still doing really well with her hunting in the large yard. When it came to Blaze though, Taxi was more of the fun police and she'd commonly tell Blaze in no uncertain terms to "knock it off". Blaze, even as an adult always respected Taxi and never challenged her.

I was still talking to Mandy on a regular basis as we had grown to be quite good friends. With things settled down in the house with Gunner, and Blaze missing Vegas so much, Mandy had started hinting that maybe Blaze needed a friend.

In early 2012, Mandy had decided to breed her red girl Flair to her black boy George who actually was Blaze's brother. As the breeding took, Mandy's hint became a little stronger!

In this case, Mandy had already determined that all the puppies in this litter would have the word "fire" in their registered names. I had made the joke that if she had a nice show red boy in the litter, I'd take him only if she'd register him under "Pants on Fire" and I could call him "Liar".

Well, the litter took, and on March 3, 2012, amongst all the puppies, a gorgeous little red boy came out and soon we added a little "Liar" to our pack!

As a puppy, Gunner was incredibly calm. He loved his toys but was particularly gentle with them, never destroying or ripping any of them. He'd have his mischievous puppy moments where he rolled around on the floor with Vegas but for the most part, the house was left unscathed with Gunner.

Blaze on the other hand, was a wild puppy! You couldn't turn your back on her for a second and even with constant watching, she left a path of unrecognizable destruction on numerous occasions. She also was a fast gulper. What I mean by that is, if she somehow grabbed a sock or something of like nature, I'd have to pretend not to notice until I was right beside her and then grab both her and the object at the same time. If I didn't do this, she'd know I was going to take her "fun" away and try to swallow it immediately!

Liar was a weird combination of both puppies. He, like Gunner, was also incredibly laid back and very rarely caused any problems. But the Blaze likeness meant he loved to pull Taxis tail and had a weird fascination for the "couch monster" and metal.

The "couch monster" was something that obviously hid between the couch cushions and would on occasion, roar out to Liar aggressively! He in turn would run full bore at the couch and in one leap land on it getting his head with his ear tapes on wedged in between the cushions on a regular basis. I'd hear a commotion of sorts and upon arriving into the living room, find this little cute Doberman butt sticking up into the air with a little nubby tail wagging aggressively.

Being supportive of his "attack", I'd let him hunt down the couch monster until I saw signs he was getting scared and stuck. I'd then ever so careful, un-wedge his head and shoulders, place him on the carpet, and together the two of us under Blazes supervision, would pull out the couch cushions off to investigate further. We never did find the couch monster, never found anything other than change that had fallen out of my pocket but it always proved to be entertaining for sure!

Liars' metal fascination was something from a different world I'm sure and was very hard on my heart.

I could be sitting on the couch watching television and little Liar would wander off to do some exploring. I didn't have to watch him like I did with Blaze when she was a puppy so I'd let him disappear for a few minutes. On occasion though, Liar would come sprinting back into the living with some form of metal hanging out of his mouth.

There is nothing more scary then seeing your beloved puppy coming running at you with a cake knife hanging out of his mouth! It's truly like a horror story!

Further to that, you didn't dare chase him or he'd sprint around the whole damn house with it!

Screw drivers, steak knives, forks, never a "safe" spoon, even a saw once that I'd left out doing some house renovations! It was mortifying as he could have killed or seriously maimed himself! This fascination became even stronger as he learned the fine art of counter surfing. Which I might add, Blaze and Gunner never counter surfed.

My typical routine was to place all the dishes in the sink and let them soak in the hot soapy water for a time while I watched television. Liar learned to satisfy his metal fascination by then bobbing in the soapy water filled sink for whatever he wanted and would then quickly bring me his various trophies.

The fear of Liar somehow stabbing himself with these sharp metal objects was terrible but he never did thank God. I will say though, it was sometimes comical to see that little soapy Santa Claus beard on him. I learned yet again to quickly adjust and all metals had to be placed in the stove until I was willing to supervise properly.

Thankfully, Liar grew out of this counter surfing sharp knife stealing phase rather quickly.

Some may question why I would have gotten another puppy with already having Gunner, Blaze and Taxi. As I said, I wanted a friend for Blaze. Blaze had so much energy and after Vegas passed, she had difficulties expending this energy.

Liar was perfect for Blaze and she quickly took on the role of being both his mom and friend. They wrestled constantly and out in the yard they chased each other for hours. I often sat on Gunner's side of the fence watching everyone and truly felt so blessed and so peaceful.

I found such joy in playing ball with Gunner and watching him lounge in his kiddie pool. Taxi was a joy to watch as she so intensely hunted all the time but sadly did catch, kill and typically eat anything she caught. Blaze and Liar would play bow to each other and rear up on their hind legs as if they were boxing.

I had mentioned a lady named Donna earlier. She was about my age, single, trained dogs as well as showed them and was owned by two beautiful labs and one gorgeous all black female German Shepherd. She lived in a small town a few hours away but after meeting her in the Rally ring, we too quickly become friends.

For the hours I spent in the yard with the pack all playing, I'd also spend a lot of the time on the cordless phone with Donna talking. We'd share training ideas, canine health problems and just life stories in general.

When we originally met, Donna's female black German Shepherd was having some medical issues. Wicca was incredibly well trained by Donna and excelled famously in the Rally ring as well as the Obedience ring. But Wicca had been diagnosed with food allergies and at times wasn't focused in training. I shared the history of course with Gunner and recommend a few times that Donna have Wicca tested for thyroid. Donna would talk to her vet and they in turn like I had, would just make adjustments to Wiccas' diet and grooming regimen.

Eventually though, Donna did finally push hard enough and did test Wicca and sure enough, she came back with also a very low thyroid. Wicca was given thyroid supplementation and as Gunner had, a lot of the symptoms resolved. Sadly though, also like Gunner both Donna and I had to wonder how much internal damage had been done while both our dogs had gone undiagnosed for so long.

Again like Gunner, Wicca was hard to stabilize with her supplementation and did for the rest of her life still have flare ups of rashes or sores that didn't heal well.

Where Gunner had aggression issues, Wicca was more inclined to just stop listening to Donna and this was evident in the Rally ring as well. Wicca could one day get a perfect score and high in class in the Excellence level of Rally which is an amazing achievement and then the next, she was like a different dog altogether! She would do well in the ring but Donna admitted she could tell Wicca didn't have her head in the game properly.

Donna and I learned to laugh these issues off as I guess we both understood each other well. Here's Donna, this great dog trainer and her own dog just seems to zone out mentally! My dog loves me incredibly and then goes from that to attacking me. Call us strange, but we had to laugh! What else could we do?

Thank God for free long distance calling because Donna and I spent hours on the phone, literally until the battery on one of our phones would die, dramatically and abruptly ending our conversations. Although we were both so content with our lives, we were both still lonely for the human companionship though.

Donna was so busy with working and taking care of her pack, and then also doing dog training that she hadn't had time to find her soul mate. With me, Gunner was outright dangerous for a while so I never even bothered or considered it. Even as things settled down with Gunner, I had so much going on now working full time again, still running the booth for Gunner and going to the dogs shows that my down time was spent working in the yard and hanging out with my pack.

Donna and I consistently joked about the old spinsters we'd become with a thousand dogs. We were both very happy, peaceful and content with our dogs, yet again, we did miss the human companionship of our unfound "soul mates".

I had taken the leap to try the whole online dating thing but the problem was that I never met anyone with who I wanted to take time out of my life to actually date. After a while of having my profile up, I decided that it was a complete waste of my time. I decided that it wasn't meant to be and was simply a destructive distraction from my happy life.

With resolution in my heart, I woke up on a Saturday morning during the long weekend in May of 2013, and with Gunner beside me on his out time, we marched to the computer to delete my profile. As I entered the dating site, this face popped up on my screen that was determined as a "match" for me. I looked in those eyes and saw a kindness and a warmth which drew me to read his profile. I read the profile out to Gunner and when I was done, I looked at Gunner and said, "This is it buddy, one more try, I'll email this guy and if he doesn't respond in a few hours, we're done!".

I typed that email, telling that stranger that I liked his profile. I told him who I was, about the pack and simply stated that I was going fishing with my dad for the day and hoped to hear from him. I sent the email and proceeded with my plans.

I drove out to mom and dads and on that fairly cold spring day, dad and I headed out in the boat to catch some fish on Netley Creek. We had, as per normal, a great time but didn't catch anything other than nasty bullheads. After a few hours of us sitting there with the occasional rain drops falling on us, we decided to call it a day and head back in. I have to admit though, off and on during our fishing trip, I caught myself thinking of that guys profile. Nobody on that dating site had ever interested me, but this guy did. I think it was his eyes.

When I returned home, I got into the house and took care of feeding and pottying the various pack members and eventually settled in. I went back to the computer, this time with Blaze following and to my surprise, I had mail! That guy wrote back!

That guy and I shared a number of back and forth emails that day and to say my heart was a little fluttery is an understatement. I couldn't believe how email talking to him was so easy. Within hours, we exchanged phone numbers and that night we made plans to meet the next day half way between our homes for our first official date!

Now people, this is online dating. I was nervous, I was even scared a little. What if he was a crazy, knife wielding, drug taking, possession stealing, and murderer type person? I called my cousin Johnny and told him of this guy and our date coming up. I gave Johnny my license plate number for tracking, the location of the public date and even this guy's phone number just in case I went missing. With Johnny's blessing and a promise to call him the minute I got home, I left on my date.

And then came Tim!

Above : Tim and Karen.
Below : Tim and his Blaze. Please note that Tim gets the
floor while Blaze uses him as a pillow from the couch.

19 ~ AND THEN CAME TIM

Tim and I had agreed on our last phone call the night before, that meeting for our first date would be best at somewhat of the halfway mark between our homes. The problem for Tim though was because of my "stranger danger" fears, I hadn't told Tim exactly where I lived. When I recommended a little diner in Lockport, Tim happily agreed believing that was in fact the halfway point.

As I pulled up to Skinner's on the old River Road in Lockport, I will admit I was terribly excited and yet so fearful! Would he even show up? Was he like his profile or was this a classic case of a lie that you hear so much about where he'd turn out to be some big burly truck driver woman? Not that big, burly truck driver women don't deserve love too, but that just wasn't my "thing".

Tim did show up and he was him! He looked exactly like he did in that picture that stole my heart only the day before!

His eyes were a brilliant sparkling blue that still take my breath away even to this day, years later. He wore a black ball cap on his clean shaven bald head and had on jeans and a nice but casual button up shirt. He looked like a good old down home relaxed country boy.

We had an awesome first date that lasted all day long!

We had our late lunch at Skinner's diner where we played music on the old jukebox at our table and as promised I serenaded him. For the record, I have a terrible singing voice which I had previously warned him about and on his dare, I belted out the song at the top of my lungs!

From there we both jumped in the Escape and took a drive to Selkirk, Manitoba and walked briefly around the boat museum. As far as the weather was concerned, it was a pretty miserable, cold, and rainy spring day but we didn't care! I was completely lost in him and felt so warm inside. There was no way a rainy spring day could ever take that feeling away. From there, we drove out to Birds Hill Park where we talked casually as we drove around aimlessly and looked for deer in the fields.

I think by the time it was all said and done, we tore through almost a full tank of gas with all our driving but it was gas well spent. I couldn't believe how relaxed everything felt with Tim. I truly felt that I'd known him all my life!

On that drive, Tim of course learned a few things about me and I about him. I did reveal where approximately, but not exactly, I lived and we still to this day laugh about it.

At the time of our first date, Tim lived in Lorette, a small town south west of Winnipeg. I, at the time, was on Calder which was just south of the town of Selkirk, but a strong north of Winnipeg. Tim quickly caught on that the diner I had picked out as the halfway mark was not so "halfway". It was a seven minute drive for me and a fifty minute drive for Tim!

The second and most important thing Tim learned about me was that yes, I liked dogs and had dogs. I had FOUR dogs, three of which were Dobermans. I also explained graphically that my blue boy was a tad "dicey" at times but overall a great dog. It seemed like a natural thing for me to tell him but I guess my presentation left a bit to be desired because Tim admitted later that where he liked me he also wasn't sure what the heck to think of the dogs!

Tim had said that he didn't have a problem with dogs in fact, he'd grown up with a German Shepherd himself so I guess I just assumed that Dobermans wouldn't be that big of a deal. What Tim didn't reveal until quite some time later though was that when he was young, he'd had a very terrifying experience with two Dobermans. These two Dobermans sat starring at him growling while he was supposed to be sleeping on a friends couch. While the dogs hadn't bit him, they still stood over him growling all night long. This had scared the crap out of Tim, which is no surprise.

We finished our long drive in Birds Hill Park and drove back to the Lockport Diner where Tim's car had been left parked. We continued to talk in the Escape though for quite some time and every time Tim laughed, my heart fluttered with butterflies!

After around six or seven hours of this first date, we agreed we should call it a day. At this point, I looked Tim straight in the eyes and said, "So this went great! I think we should take our profiles down, I've finally found you!" I don't quite remember Tim's reply but I do know we agreed to a second date and in my heart, I knew he was the one!

I can look anyone in the eye and say that I never believed in love at first sight and it's true! On the contrary, I very much believed that love happens over time as people get to know each other. When I'd hear about love at first sight, quite frankly, I thought it was garbage.

I left the parking lot first with Tim following in his car behind me. When we got to highway #44, I turned left to go home and Tim turned right to head back to his home in Lorette. As I watched his car drive away in my rearview mirror, my heart sank and the tears started flowing. He was the one! I remember thinking, will I ever see him again? I was both so excited and so scared all at the same time.

I got home from our date and immediately called my cousin Johnny to let him know that Tim wasn't that crazy, drug taking, possession stealing, murderer type guy and that I was safe. As Johnny picked up the phone, all I could say was in my excitement was, "Cuz, I finally found him! He's exactly him! I always knew who it would be but just never knew his name and now I do! It's Tim."

Both my cousin and I cried happy tears during that phone call at my happiness and I remember Johnny saying, "I've said prayers to God for you cuz that you'd find him. I'm so happy for you!"

Tim and I had our second date very soon after the first and it too went fabulous. I took him fishing which was a big part of my life over by mom and dads house on Netley creek. We caught oodles of Walleye, Sauger and Bull Head and had a complete blast yet again and my thoughts of Tim being the one were quickly coming true. Everything seemed so natural with him and I was sure the last hurdle of meeting the dogs would go just as well.

We agreed that the third date would be a supper at my place so he could meet the pack that he'd heard so much about. As Tim pulled up at the house, I had Blaze, Liar and Taxi all in their kennels and Gunner was on his out time. As Tim got out of his car and proceeded to the gate, I let Gunner out and he of course bolted out of the house like a rocket and ran straight to the gate to "greet" Tim.

I can honestly say that I didn't see any fear at all on Tim's face but I know now that he was hiding it with all his might. As Tim described later, this massive Doberman who had attacked me before came flying out of the house at him. He still hadn't told me about his previous Doberman experience but even with Gunner flying at him, Tim still opened the gate and started walking up the sidewalk towards us. Gunner quickly spun around, ran back into the house and then came flying out again with a toy hanging out of his mouth. Before you knew it, Gunner and Tim were playing fetch!

For supper, Tim and I had agreed to have a lovely steak bar-b-que and while Tim cooked on the grill, I'd make the salad and potatoes. I remember vividly Tim going out onto the deck to prepare the bar-b-que and Gunner following right behind. I could tell that Gunner had immediately taken to Tim and Gunner was in an amazing mood!

I stood at the kitchen island making the salad when in came Tim and in such a calm voice he politely asked, "Do you have a small garbage bag? There's a little situation with the bar-b-que."

As much as I could try to remember, I had no idea when or even if I had used that bar-b-que in the last few years. Turns out, they make lovely condo apartments for mice, squirrels or what have you and there was a monster nest of some sort in my bar-b-que!

Again Tim and I laughed and he ever so casually cleaned out the nest, disinfected and de-contaminated the bar-b-que all while still playing fetch with Gunner.

We had a fabulous dinner and when we went to settle down in the living room to talk on the couch, I changed the pack up putting Gunner in his large living room kennel and letting out Taxi, Blaze and Liar.

As Tim sat on the couch waiting for these other dogs, again I saw no fear and didn't really think at all about how overwhelming it could be. I knew they were great dogs and let's face facts, my only concern was really the Gunner meeting and that had gone fabulous!

Taxi tromped her way in wagging her long spindly matted tail, Liar immediately jumped onto the loveseat where he knew I'd be siting but Blaze was the surprise!

I'd said before that Blaze wasn't a snuggly dog, she wasn't at all ever in her life. She never sat close to me, never wanted to be petted really and while I knew she was fond of me, she never really showed any real closeness to me.

Coming out of her kennel, Blaze went straight to Tim and immediately started nudging him for pats which shocked me. After he petted her a few times, she jumped up on the couch right beside him and flopped down hard, sprawling out across his lap and actually wanted a belly rub! You could have knocked me over with a feather at this! She had never wanted belly rubs from me.

They say that dogs are a good judge of character and I've always believed that. In this case, it was quickly obvious to me that I wasn't the only one who had the "love at first sight" experience. Blaze had found her true love as well!

Blaze was actually somewhat embarrassing as she moaned and groaned loudly with every pat that Tim gave her. She looked absolutely attention deprived! That night, we sat in the living room talking and Blaze laid sprawled out across Tim the whole time. I normally would have changed the dogs up again but I was happy for Blaze, she was in seventh heaven and I didn't want it to stop for her!

Tim and I have literally broken every rule possible when it's come to what the "experts" say on successful dating and relationships.

We had our first date on the May long weekend of 2013 and did both remove our online dating profiles soon after. In that August, Tim moved into my house on Calder as it made sense for the dogs as he was in a Condo in Lorette. That Christmas, Tim got me a beautiful promise ring followed by an engagement ring the Christmas after that.

As we shared our life stories, it was amazing how many times our paths had crossed but we just never actually met. I guess this too confirms the "when it's meant to be, it'll be" line. We both think we just weren't quite ready to meet yet.

Tim told me about his bad Doberman experience eventually and it amazed me as he immediately attached so well to the dogs and they to him. Can you imagine having such a terrible experience and then being asked to walk into a house with three Dobermans? I'm a die-hard dog person, and I don't know if I would have been able to do it.

Add to that, while Tim said he liked dogs and had them growing up, none of them ever lived in the house with him. This doesn't mean he wasn't close to them. He was very close to his German Shepherd but he stayed outside, as that was how Tim was raised.

In our home, our 985sq foot tiny home, Tim was constantly saying the command "beep beep" to get around dogs. Dog toys were strewn about the house, dogs were strewn about the furniture and simply, dogs were everywhere it seemed all the time! I had explained how many people called the Dobermans "Velcro dogs" and Tim quickly learned this particularly with Blaze as she was now always beside him.

Tim couldn't even take a bath without his Blaze nudging the door open, only to walk in and sit beside the tub staring at him or dropping toys into the tub. This can be incredibly overwhelming and privacy invading but Tim took to it very well and learned if he wanted or needed privacy, doors had to be shut tight. Sadly though, if he did shut the doors tight, there would then be whining on the other side of the door which of course pulled at Tim's heart strings.

I'll admit, with Taxi, after watching her catch, kill and eat things that commonly got stuck in her whiskers, I didn't snuggle her much anymore but Tim always did and always spoke Spanish to her or English with a Spanish accent.

Taxi, like Blaze, commonly jumped on Tim's lap for snuggles and Tim obliged even if she stank to high heaven from rolling in dead stuff. Every time Taxi approached Tim, he'd say with his poor Spanish, "Hola chica, como estas" and Taxi as if she understood would wag her tail and put her two little front paws up on him. Tim would then reach down, pat Taxi quite vigorously and when she walked away satisfied with the pats, he'd quickly go wash his hands. When I asked Tim why the Spanish he just said she looked like she spoke it. I have to admit, I'd never "seen" that before with Taxi, but yeah, she sort of did look like she might speak Spanish. That is of course if a dog was able to talk.

I had explained to Tim in great detail that although I hadn't had problems with Gunner in quite some time, he still had issues and could be dicey. Tim and Gunner hit it off famously and Tim learned very quickly to recognize the "eyes" of Gunner and when he'd need to be kenneled. There were a few occasions where Tim did see this and did get Gunner into his kennel preventing any outbursts.

Liar and Blaze seemed to make their own decision when it came to how things were going to be in our home now with Tim. Blaze was now "daddy's little girl" and Liar even though he liked Tim very much accepted Blazes decision and quickly came to be "mommy's sucky baby boy".

While Tim and I wanted to snuggle with each other while watching movies, this rarely happened because Blaze was always on Tim's lap and even trained him to have a pillow for her. So, Tim and Blaze got the couch and Liar and I got the loveseat. Taxi shared her affections with both of us and bounced back and forth between the couch and loveseat and Gunner had his large kennel beside Tim and Blaze.

The amazing story comes with Blaze though and truly warms my heart. Don't get me wrong, she's always been a great girl but was always stand offish as if something was missing for her. Liar was a great addition to Blazes life and brought her a little out of this shell so to speak. With Tim though, she literally changed before my eyes, from this stand offish girl to a girl who couldn't get enough snuggle time with him and I loved watching every minute of it!

Tim says to this day that Blaze was his first Doberman friend and always says it with a smile beaming on his face! The two of them have a connection that cannot be explained in words. Blaze's eyes light up the minute she sees her Tim and her little nub wags constantly when he talks to her or when he's even just in the same room.

Tim does comment from time to time on how he wishes he was closer with Liar but Blaze simply won't allow it. Liar will climb on Tim's lap for snuggles but after a few minutes Blaze barks as if to tell them both to knock it off. Liar will jump down, Tim apologizes to Blaze and she jumps up with the strongest love in her eyes that I've ever seen.

When we met, Tim was working for a cement and concrete company which leads to winter layoffs of employment. The two of us had decided quite quickly in our relationship that while we enjoyed living in Calder, we'd truly like to be living on the water somewhere. Further to that, with four dogs and us two humans, Calder was now seeming to be a pretty small house.

With Tim's winter layoff coming, we decided we would start renovations on Calder to ready it for sale. This left Tim alone with the pack while I was at work during the winter and during this time Tim also strongly bonded with Gunner. But how could he not? Gunner constantly flashed those loving squinty eyes at Tim and Gunner had so much character.

Tim felt sorry for Gunner being by himself all the time but understood also how he couldn't be trusted with the other dogs. Tim admitted though that my "rule" of switching the dogs around every hour for out time sometimes wasn't followed though because he felt Gunner needed a little more attention.

My family all adored Tim and they too, quickly connected with him. My cousin Johnny who was more like my brother "adopted" Tim as his brother and the two of them get along amazingly.

My dad spent his whole life in construction to where he had to medically retire as the Superintendent of a large construction company in Manitoba. Upon hearing about the renovations going on at Calder, Dad quickly volunteered his help and provided guidance to Tim which he accepted and the two of them also became very close.

Before I met Tim, I had so many conversations with Aunty Dee, Donna and my cousin Johnny about me being single and although I wasn't alone because of the dogs, I was alone. I had so many joys in my life and I wanted so badly to have someone with whom I could run into their open arms and share those joyful moments with. I also wanted to share those not so happy times with someone. If I had a rough day, I wanted to feel that safeness in someone's arms. While the dogs kept me company and I adored them, I still wanted that feeling of being safe in the arms of the one you love. That was something I couldn't get from the dogs. But now I had it finally with Tim.

In my heart, I do believe in God and where I don't go to church, I pray a lot and have a very strong belief. I prayed so many times to God that he would show me my soul mate. I did give up on finding my soul mate, and I can say I wasn't angry or bitter but just resolved in the fact that it wasn't going to happen. Even without my soul mate, I was truly blessed in my life with all the dogs, the home, the land, how could I not feel blessed? But I did find him!

I often tell Tim, "I always knew you, I just had to wait for the right time to find you and learn your name."

It's so very true, Tim is my soul mate!

Above : Taxi on the deck at Calder.
Below : Old timer Vegas

20 ~ TAXI

Tim and I have always believed that everything happens for a reason and we still believe this now to this day. In the moment that something happens, particularly something negative, you may not understand the reason but as time goes on, you learn why it happened and the answers reveal themselves.

Take for example that first email I sent to Tim on the May long weekend in 2013. The minute I had sent it, I vowed to Gunner that if this guy didn't write back in the next few hours, I was going to delete my profile and get off that dating site. I'll say right now, I would have followed through and deleted my profile never to return to that dating site again!

The funny thing is, every long weekend in May, Tim always went out to stay at a friend's fishing lodge in Ontario. Because of the miserable weather and the ice coming off Lake of the Woods harshly, the fishing lodge had suffered ice damages and Tim couldn't go out that fateful year in 2013.

That was the first May long weekend Tim had missed going in about twenty years and he was quite upset about that. But, that was the weekend we met. If he'd gone like all the years before, he would have missed my email and it's quite possible this would be a completely different book and we'd both have had completely different lives! Hmmm, funny how that worked out!

So with everything happening for a reason, Tim and I spent our first spring and summer together learning about each other and being in new found love. It was an amazing time for us of constant change, learning and growth.

Both of us were in our early 40's and let's just say that by that age, you've grown accustomed to living life a certain way and doing things a certain way. With two people merging into each other's lives, everything's different and common ground has to be found or you simply won't make it as a unit. But Tim and I worked together through these differences and adapted to each other quickly. It's not to say we didn't have hiccups so to speak, but we vowed to each other to figure it out together.

The dogs quickly trained Tim to fit in with us. And I do mean they trained him! I don't think he'd be willing to admit it but those dogs had him totally wrapped around their paws and I loved watching Tim learn from them.

Gunner trained Tim to constantly throw the spit covered Cuz he always seemed to have in his mouth. No matter how much spit was on that Cuz, Tim always threw it because if he didn't, Gunner would drop it in his lap and forcefully nudge his groin area until he did throw it! It's amazing how fast you get over handling a spit covered toy when you've got a large male Doberman nudging you in the crotch.

Gunner also trained Tim to help him when that Cuz fell inside the house too close to the vacuum cleaner for Gunner himself to safely retrieve. It was funny to watch because we could be watching television while Gunner squeaked in the background and when I'd see the Cuz land by the vacuum, I'd start to watch the two of them and the interaction.

Gunner would stare at the vacuum waiting for it to lunge at him because we all know vacuum cleaners lunge aggressively and then he'd glance at Tim who was engrossed in the movie. Gunner would start by making a "huffing" sound which Tim typically wouldn't hear or would maybe pretend not to hear. He'd then graduate to a light bark. With Tim not taking his eyes off the television, he'd get up, go to the vacuum, pick up the Cuz and hand it to Gunner saying, "Here you go buddy". Tim would then return to the couch and continue watching the show while Gunner commenced his annoying relentless squeaking.

Blaze trained Tim in the fine art of snuggles. It was always about snuggling and petting with Blaze, as she adored this from Tim. If he was standing outside talking, she'd sneak up tight and lean against him and start nudging his hand as it hung by his side. Without him even noticing, Tim would start petting his Blaze. The minute he stopped, she'd nudge him again and he'd go back to petting her.

As I said with the couch, Tim was trained very quickly that before Blaze sprawled out on him, he always needed to have the couch pillow ready for her to comfortably rest her head on while she laid on him. During this snuggle time it was truly about her. Blaze knew Tim had two hands and they both best be petting her at all times. And not just resting on her but actively petting.

If Tim tried to talk on the phone he quickly received "stink eye" from Blaze followed by sad groans and aggressive nudges that escalated to the point where he simply couldn't talk on the phone anymore.

I don't know how Taxi did it, but she truly had Tim wrapped around her paw! Even though I regularly bathed Taxi, she always rolled in nasty stuff and stank to high heaven. She was sixteen or seventeen now and was having booboos in her kennel from time to time, but Tim overlooked it saying he'd probably be the same in his old age. He still snuggled Taxi regularly but always felt like he had to change his clothes or at least wash his hands after. He still spoke to her in Spanish but started calling her "Mangy Critter" as his term of endearment for her.

Out of all the dogs though, Tim and Taxi did "scrap" on a regular basis. Taxi continued to hunt and kill animals in the yard and always deposited the bodies under the farthest part of the deck. That part of the deck only had about a foot and half clearance so as much as Tim tried, he could never get under there to clean it out. Further to that, it was in an area that was constantly hit by direct sunlight and also right by our back door which was our main point of entrance.

The combination of dead "something" and heat made for a very overwhelming stench greeting any and all people who came by to visit. While you can get used to certain things or smells, even just trying to come or go from our own home was an issue with this persistent stench. In particular, this drove Tim crazy but sadly there was very little we could do. Pre-Tim, I just always held my breath as I bolted into the house as there was no way in hell I was going to try crawling under that nasty deck!

With Tim and my cousin Johnny getting so close, we'd gotten into the habit of having Johnny and his wife Dawn over for a night on the weekends. We'd typically order in, bar-b-que, or at least have some sort of meal and then settle in for the evening with music, a few drinks and a few rounds of dice.

On one occasion in the late fall, Johnny and Dawn had come over and Johnny was sporting his new look of crutches due to a severe ankle break he'd recently suffered that required extensive surgery.

As Johnny, with his big frame hobbled up the three stairs to get onto the deck, Dawn and I stood ready on either side of him to catch him should he loose his balance. He cleared the stairs just fine but we'd had a light rain and as he made his way across the wood deck he slipped and fell hard.

I had turned away from Johnny to get the door and I can remember the impact of him falling vividly as it actually bounced me on the deck and made a terrible "thud" sound!

Tim was on his way home from being in Winnipeg so this left Dawn and I trying to scoop Johnny up and get him into the house. Thankfully, we did get him in and although he was incredibly sore, he didn't feel any extra damage had been done. Tim arrived home shortly thereafter and was completely mortified that Johnny had fallen. We continued our evening as planned though and as always, had a wonderful time!

A few weeks later in the middle of the night, with the dogs all sleeping and the room dark, I was awoken by Tim whispering, "Karen, are you awake?"

Well I wasn't at the time but was now. "Yes baby, what's wrong? Everything okay?"

"I have a confession…. I can't sleep, I have to tell you something and it's bad," he said sounding so incredibly serious.

I now sat up, Tim seemed so terribly upset. "What's wrong baby?"

"Well, 'member the night that Johnny fell on the deck?"

"Yeah…."

"It stank so badly from Taxi, and I couldn't get the dead stuff out and I didn't want Johnny and Dawn smelling all that. So I read online about a deodorizer spray that I could make. You take laundry soap and water and mix it together with some other stuff. I did that and put it in that big sprayer we have and I tried spraying that area where Taxi leaves the dead animals. But I think I got it on the deck because I couldn't get it all between the boards. I think the over spray made the deck slippery and that's why he fell!"

I couldn't stop laughing! The more I laughed, the more upset Tim got. All I could keep saying was, "You soaped the deck on Johnny?!?"

Needless to say, Tim had felt absolutely terrible about all this and had carried it for weeks. He felt so bad that Johnny had fallen that it was literally eating him up inside!

My cousin Johnny and I are really close and have been for years. We're also both known to have somewhat of a morbid sense of humor that not many understand and we tend to laugh at things that many say aren't humorous.

I thought Tim soaping the deck was hilarious and I knew Johnny would think so too, especially since time had passed and Johnny hadn't hurt himself further with the fall. I strongly urged Tim to confess to him so as to clear his conscience but Tim was nervous about that as he didn't want Johnny thinking he'd done it on purpose.

Finally at a wedding social that we all attended and after Johnny and Tim had a few drinks in them, Tim started his confession. He never got to finish his whole confession because Johnny caught on and kept saying, "So my brother, let me see if I understand you, you soaped the deck?!? I have titanium shit in my ankle and you soaped the deck?"

Johnny, Dawn and I were all laughing so hard! It took Tim a bit to understand the humor! Well, I'm not sure that he has to this day completely, but we thought it was hilarious! And as a side note, that spray did work miracles covering up that dead thing smell!

Taxi and Tim had the ongoing "dead things stinking under the deck" fight all summer long and into the fall. Taxi would drag something under there and Tim would spend the afternoon trying to drag it out before it started to stink. Taxi usually won the battle though as she was so quick, half the time we didn't even know she had dragged anything under there until a few days had passed and we'd start to notice the flies and smell.

I have to say, I never thought it possible to have so much character and chaos wrapped into such a teeny tiny body as Taxi did. You hear "Doberman" and I think one tends to think big, burly, aggressive dogs but Taxi ran them. She truly was the highest dog on the totem pole and not once did any of the Dobermans challenge her. Please remember, she packed all that feistiness into maybe 8 lbs of fur!

That year, Taxi was sixteen or seventeen years old and I had started to call her "my little Sophia Petrillo" from Golden Girls.

Taxi would wake up some mornings full of piss and vinegar and head out hunting, killing and telling the Dobermans what to do and how fast to do it. Other mornings though, she woke up and seemed to be barely living at all and acting like her next breath would be her last, just like that Sophia. Tim and I called it "fake dying" because just when we'd think we'd have to take her into the vet, she'd bounce right back and start hunting again. We did notice though that Liar had started to sniff Taxi a lot. Not her butt like normal dog sniffing, but he'd sniff her body and I worried that cancer was setting in.

This went on all summer and fall of that year, and we did notice that Taxi had started to lose weight and my fear of cancer was getting stronger. As feisty as she could be sometimes, you could tell her time was coming. I was nervous about this as I knew I'd take it hard and this wasn't something Tim and I had been through together yet. I knew he had grown fond of Taxi but I also knew I'd have real difficulties with it and didn't know if Tim would be supportive. I mean, I thought he would but you never know until you're in that moment, how people deal with death.

Sadly mid-January of 2014, Tim and I decided after three days of "fake dying" that this time, Taxi wasn't going to come back from it and together, Tim and I took that "mangy little critter" into the vet for her final visit.

Tim held me close as the vet examined Taxi and concurred that it was time. Tim and I cried together and patted her gently as we watched Taxi's little eyes close for the last time.

I did have a rough time loosing Taxi and Tim was amazing through this period. He was surprised himself though at how hard he took it. He only knew Taxi for less than a year but he admitted that she had stolen a big part of his heart and he had a lot of respect for her, how she "bossed Blaze and Liar around".

I was so blessed to have Tim to help me through this and thanked God for him.

I haven't really discussed Vegas' passing in this book and I'll do it here for reasons you'll understand later. You may opt to skip the rest of this chapter as it may seem morbid but if you've never had to let go of one of your canine best friends, you may find this next bit helpful in removing at least some of the fears.

Years before when I had to put Isaac, my beloved German Shepherd down, I was terrified at the thought. I think the "unknown" is at times most crippling. I had no idea how it was done or what would happen or even what to expect.

I had discussed with my vet beforehand, how the whole procedure would go and together we had a plan of how it would be handled.

Please know, you have options on this final stage of your pets' life! Some choose to stay in the room with their pet and others leave, the choice is yours and you can't be judged for it as everyone deals with their grief differently. You can choose what you want done with your pets' body and this should also be discussed beforehand so you don't have to deal with it in your time of grief.

Some choose to leave the body with the vet and the vet can send it for cremation and return the ashes to you in an urn that you've picked out. Others may take the body so as they can bury their friend. The vets, upon your direction, can also just take the body and dispose of it themselves. You do have choices.

With Isaac, I went into the operatory with him, taking one of his blankets. I carefully laid the blanket out on the floor, sat on it with my Aunty Dee and had Isaac lay down with his head in my lap.

As I patted Isaac the whole time, the vet gave Isaac a sedative and then warned me before he injected him with the agent that would cease Isaac's life. I again have tears flowing down my cheeks as I write this, but it's important because I want you to know that it was very calm, loving and very peaceful. My Isaac seemed to gently fall asleep in my lap and drift away from me. When I was ready, I left Isaac on his blanket and a few days later the vet gave me his ashes in an urn I still have today.

When Vegas' time came, he was a very nervous dog and I wanted to do my best to make him as comfortable as possible. He now, in his old age, and without Isaac absolutely hated car rides and always hyperventilated during our travels. The vets office was at least a forty five minute drive and with Vegas not doing well to begin with, I wanted to avoid the car ride altogether.

I had heard of a vet that would come to your home and I felt that this would be better for Vegas to feel the comfort of Blaze and Taxi around. Many had also said that if you have other dogs, that it is good for them to see as they then know and understand when their friend has left them.

What I didn't know was that this vet handled the whole procedure differently.

The vet did come to my home and in the living room, I had Vegas on my lap snuggling. She gave Vegas a light sedative that made him groggy as opposed to make him fall asleep. His eyes rolled around and he started crying in what seemed like confusion or fear. The vet then rolled him on his back, which Vegas did start to try to struggle against. She then proceeded to inject a needle straight into his heart which took his life, but he did yelp. I've had nightmares about that as it was not peaceful! In my opinion it had fear and I think pain and where I was trying to do right by Vegas, I think he left me feeling consumed with fear. It breaks my heart to write that, but I think it's true and I will never forget it!

Taxi's procedure I had also talked to the vet about and it was very "peaceful" like Isaac's was. Both Tim and I knew what to expect and while you're never "ready", we were at least ready, or prepared, is the better word as to what would happen. I write this because please discuss it with your vet beforehand so that you don't have surprises in your grief may effect you for the rest of your life.

Make a plan that is peaceful and humane because the time will come that you may have to make that decision for your best friend to ease them of their pain.

Above : Blaze wearing Tim's ice fishing cap.
Below : Liar, bringing my cousin Johnny some duct tape.

21 ~ WHO LET THE DOGS OUT?

"Quirk" is defined in the dictionary as being "an unusual habit or part of someone's personality, or something that is strange and unexpected". I know some feel that the word "quirk" has a negative connotation but I've always seen it as a positive. A quirk is something that separates us from each other and in my mind, makes us unique and individually beautiful.

I find it funny how certain dogs can bring quirks out of their humans that never seemed to be there before and vice versa for that matter. I wonder, is it because of these quirks that we connect sometimes deeper than other times? Or is it because of the connection that we have that we develop the quirks? Maybe it's the old age question of which came first, the chicken or the egg?

If we're lucky enough, we notice these "special" quirks and we foster them into what becomes some of our most favorite memories! In doing so, we recognize that while many dogs in our lives may have had similar traits, each of them has their own special "quirks" that no other dog does just like they do.

I have spent most of my life training dogs, sometimes at a professional level but mostly for simple day to day living. One thing that most "animal trainers" will agree on is that dogs, in particular, want to please their owners and learn by a reward system. By utilizing the right balance of praise and reward for desirable actions and ignoring or disciplining the bad behaviors, you will achieve this to various levels.

Taking into account what your dog brings with him or her "to the table", and how you work with them I believe, will allow you both to expand your horizons so to speak.

Gunner brought many different things to the table that I recognized I wanted to bring out as a puppy. He had a cute calmness about him that surprised me for a puppy. It started simply in just the way he woke up. He never just woke up ready to start his day with vigor. He lounged himself awake and this is something I can honestly say I'd never experienced before. To me, this was Gunner's first cute little quirk.

Case in point with Blaze, she can go to bed for the evening and in the morning when the alarm goes off, she goes from sound asleep to fully awake in less than a second. By the time you get to her kennel, she's already doing circles ready to take on the day.

With Gunner, the wake up process took at least ten to twenty minutes which was so much also my personality. He started off with slow yawning, a state of prolonged grogginess, and a deep stretching. Slowly, he'd stretch out to me and nuzzle his nose against my face. This became our little routine of "Wake up…. Wake up little Gunner-roo" which I so enjoyed.

That wake up routine was the foundation of our days starting out "right" and developed into his squinty eyes behavior that became adored by so many. That squinty eyed smile quirk became "a Gunner thing" that would melt anyone's heart. The more I fostered it, the more he learned it "pleased" me and in turn the more he used it sometimes to just get his own way.

The button pushing quirk was endearing originally and therefore I fostered it in the beginning. It got a tad out of control but grew out of his recognition that using it rewarded him in a multitude of ways. Sometimes it did please me, and at other times, not so much, but overall, it did reward him.

I once read about a man who had a dog that consistently got into the garbage. When talking to a trainer the trainer asked him what he did when his dog got into the garbage. The owner replied that he would "kick the dog's ass". The trainer asked if the "ass kicking" was working and the owner replied that it definitely wasn't because the dog kept doing it. The trainer asked what the reward for the dog was and the owner replied honestly that it was left over food of various kinds. The trainer pointed out that the dog was getting a treasure trove of food and it only cost him an "ass kicking" therefore, the reward was definitely worth it to the dog. When the owner asked how to stop this negative behavior, the trainer said flatly, "put the garbage up where the dog can't get it."

While dogs want primarily to please us, they also value reward and if the reward is higher to them than the actual pleasing us, they will dis-please us and be willing to suffer the ramifications for that reward.

I had lived with Gunner for five years before meeting Tim and had gone through so much with him. Through our training together, we achieved such an incredible closeness and bond, that this is what helped me push through the difficult times as opposed to giving up.

I want to be clear on "training". When I talk of training, I don't mean to say that you can only have a bond with your dog if you train him or her to heel exactly perfectly at your side. Training to me means teaching as well as learning from that dog how to live your lives in harmony.

Whether it's teaching your pup to sit nicely at the door and ring a bell to go outside, or having that same dog learning to spin like a top in front of you to signify the same thing. It's both training because the end result is the same, you don't want your dog peeing in the house for ever.

With all my dogs, I have always had unique things that I only did with them and none of the others. I learned quickly what pleased Gunner as "rewards" but just as quickly, Gunner recognized what pleased me as "rewards". We both used those rewards and fostered it and in so, trained each other.

I had mentioned some time back that I always thought the trick of "shake a paw" was silly. I'll admit, I thought that because so many dogs were taught it, that the trick was somewhat "beneath" my dogs and so therefore I refused to teach it.

Upon Tim's arrival into our family, one of the first things Tim tried was to get all the dogs to shake a paw. With none of them being taught this "trick" they all looked at him like he had two heads. But this was perfect as I gave it to Tim as a challenge that he readily accepted.

Gunner was the quickest study of "shake a paw" followed soon after by Liar. This trick always proved to be beneath Taxi. Blaze, as much as she loved and wanted to please Tim, took months to figure it out. Tim realized though, this was because he tried training them all to do it the same way and simply they all learned differently.

Tim also taught the dogs to dish out kisses, bark on command, and a variety of other tricks I hadn't spent time on. This helped Tim and the dogs bond as they learned from each other. This is also where Blaze's "thinking clack" quirk became more evident and noticeable.

My dad had always said that one of the things that separates us from dogs is the ability to think or rationalize. After watching Tim and Blaze train each other, there is no question in my mind that dogs think! Take the multitude of sessions with Blaze and the "shake a paw". Tim would patiently sit by the kitchen table with a treat in his hand and ask Blaze to shake her paw. She'd sit patiently and look back and forth from him to the treat in his hand and clack her teeth together.

Tim would pick up her paw, shake it, and then provide her with the treat. This went on for months, the exact same ritual and where it had worked in seconds on Gunner and days on Liar, Blaze wasn't "getting it". Watching them on the umpteenth training session I mentioned to Tim, "she thinks the trick is her allowing you to pick up her paw so she sits and clacks because it's taking you forever to do it."

With this, Tim adjusted and had Liar sit beside Blaze. He asked Liar to shake his paw and immediately he did and was rewarded with the treat. Tim then looked at Blaze and did the same thing only didn't pick up her paw. She didn't offer it so she got nothing and he went back to Liar who quickly offered his paw and was again rewarded. This happened a few times and Blazes clacking increased until finally Tim asked her to shake a paw, she clacked, looked at Liar, and then offered Tim her paw!

Tim, in short time learned how to teach the dogs and they also learned how to teach Tim. The exciting thing was that Tim brought out new and exciting quirks in the dogs that I so enjoyed seeing. Things that I didn't know existed and I believe that it was only Tim that could have brought these quirks out.

One of Gunner's big things with me which I found so cute was his "fake stalking". He had started this as a very young pup but with age and my "pleasure" of it, he mastered the fine art and it truly was a sight to see.

I would be working in the large yard and all of a sudden I'd feel a weird sense of being watched. As they say, you become overwhelmed in this eerie feeling and the hairs stand straight up on your neck. This would happen and I'd slowly stand up from whatever I was doing and as I turned, I would notice Gunner sometimes up to a hundred feet away staring at me and yes, stalking me!

He'd look so very darned serious, taking small, slow deliberate steps, creeping if you will, while never taking his eyes off me. I could tell it was a game because although he looked so intense, his ears would be up and pointing at my direction. I'd seen him stalk leaves and such before and during this serious stalking his ears would be pinned back in what I referred to as his "stealth mode". But when it came to stalking me, his ears would be straight up and alert.

Seeing Gunner stalk, I'd start to crouch over also going into stalking mode and he'd stop immediately, sometimes even with one of his front paws still in the air. If he stopped, I would stop. Slowly, the two of us would again start stalking each other with the space between us shortening.

This would carry on for sometimes ten to fifteen minutes as we were both so careful so as the other one not notice us moving but eventually one of us would "crack" under the pressure. This would result in Gunner breaking into a full out sprint at me with his tongue now hanging out of the side of his mouth as if in a stupid grin. When he reached me, I would roar loudly and he'd leap to the side of me but I could usually spin just in time to lovingly swat his backside.

As much fun as Tim and Gunner had in the yard together I knew it was only a matter of time until Tim was completely welcomed by Gunner into the family and he was officially stalked. I warned Tim about the stalking because if you didn't know, it looked pretty serious and very intimidating and given Gunner's past, may be taken the wrong way.

I remember the day that Tim came into the house and he was laughing so hard because for the first time Gunner had stalked him and did exactly what I said!

When Tim or I needed some down time and retreated upstairs to the bed to watch a movie, Gunner would typically join us. He'd stand at the edge of the bed with his chin on it and just do a very light little "woo... wooooooo". Upon us granting him permission to come up, he'd quickly grab his toy and join us at the foot end.

As the movie would go on and Gunner would get bored, he'd look for ways to get our attention. This would start by Gunner placing his toy on the very edge of the bed. He'd then stare at us, stare at the toy, stare at us and then back to his toy. If no one did anything, Gunner would ever so slightly nudge his toy until it fell off the bed and onto the floor.

This is what I referred to as Gunner's version of fetch. He'd stare at his toy on the floor and cry so sadly. At first it would be very light whining but if we ignored Gunner, he'd get louder and louder until we finally reached onto the floor and gave him back his toy. He'd be so excited that he had his toy back! Within seconds though, he'd again perch it right at the very edge and start the whole fetch thing again.

We knew darn well he was working us with that trick but we allowed it because it was so darn cute. How he actually thought in his mind that we didn't know what was happening or going on. So tell me, do dogs think? If you saw Gunner perch that toy right at the very edge and play the game he did, you would not question it!

Tim and Gunner through that winter of work layoff got incredibly close in a very short time until soon, they too had their special games together. Their favorite which they played all the time was "Hide and Go Seek".

I'm not sure how it started with the two of them, maybe it was a graduation from the stalking or tag but it was played only in the house.

Calder was a pre-war house and "open concept" living space was not at all in the thoughts of home builders. Calder was more of a "million small rooms shoved into a tiny house" concept. With this, Gunner would go into the living room and stare at Tim trying to get the game of Hide and Go Seek started and Tim would quickly oblige.

Tim would tell Gunner to sit where he was in the living room and then proceed to hide either in the main floor bedroom, the bathroom, behind the island in the kitchen or even in the upstairs or downstairs stairwell. When I'd see that Tim was ready, I'd ask Gunner, "Where's daddy?" and immediately Gunner would start stalking and looking for Tim.

Gunner would be moving so slowly and yet so determined to find Tim that his whole body would start to quiver with each step. Gunner would continue peeking around corners until finally Tim would jump out from behind one with a huge "ROAR!" Gunner would literally jump up straight up on his hind legs, spin around, tuck his butt under him so it couldn't be swatted and he'd sprint back to the living room!

While Gunner was sprinting to the living room, Tim would be hiding again in a new spot this time. Once Gunner reached the "safe zone" of the living room, he'd be panting wildly but would immediately sit and while grinning from ear to ear, he would be waiting for me to ask him again "Where's daddy?" This game always made me laugh because you could tell that when Tim jumped out, it did in fact scare the heck out of Gunner but oddly enough Gunner loved this game and would play it for hours if he could!

Outside in the yard, Tim, Gunner and I stuck to the stalking and games of tag. Gunner loved being chased and would constantly check over his shoulder to make sure that Tim was still following and upon noticing that Tim wasn't, Gunner would spin and chase after him. It would lead to a near collision but at the very last second, Gunner would veer off and Tim or I, would again swat or try to pinch Gunner's behind as he flew by.

Gunner and I had played tag on a number of occasions but I wasn't nearly as fast as Tim so therefore it wasn't as much fun. Our game of tag typically resulted in me getting tagged by Gunner and him ripping a few holes in my jacket with him either shoving me or taking a little love nip.

Pre-Tim, I had learned very early on with Gunner that for whatever reason, he was very fond of the song "Who Let the Dogs' Out" by Baha Men. I guess this came on because every time I let the dogs out, I'd start singing that song. In no time, upon hearing that, Gunner had taken up howling to it.

He got so good at it that I in fact made that my "alarm" on my blackberry for wake up in the morning. While I couldn't actually hear my alarm go off or that song playing, I would hear Gunner start to cry and howl in his kennel beside the bed. Learning this simply became habit that worked very effective for my hearing problems.

When Tim came into our lives, he brought his guitar which he plays incredibly well given he was self-taught. His whole family is very musically talented and quite often when they sit down together to break bread, soon after, they all break out their guitars or Dobros. While they play together old country gospel songs, others that can't play, sing along.

Tim soon started playing his guitar in our home regularly to unwind and for our first Christmas I bought him an electric acoustic Fender which the dogs and I really enjoyed. The minute they saw him pick it up in the living room, they'd all settle in to listen to the concert he'd play for them which ranged from Johnny Cash, Elvis, Gospel songs to even Gun's and Roses. But Gunner again trained Tim to start playing his favorite song "Who Let the Dogs Out" and while Tim played his heart out, Gunner would throw his head straight back and howl like he'd never howled before!

I know sometimes they say that dogs will howl to music because it actually hurts their ears but I don't believe this because of what I saw in Gunner. The minute he saw Tim pick up his guitar, he'd start whining until Tim played "their song" and he could howl. It got to the point that Tim would actually play Gunner's song first otherwise Gunner would whine and pace until he did. After Gunner was finished his "singing", he'd settle down and even fall into a very deep sleep, sucking on one of his toys while Tim played the rest of his music.

It may not seem like much, but one of our so cherished memories is of a video we have of both Tim and Gunner singing together in howling harmony. When either of us hear this on the radio even today we call each other and share our fond memories. This of course leads us to sharing so many other of the memories we have and while we laugh, we shed tears over those days gone by.

As for Gunner, never in his life did he ever sing to any other song except on one occasion while driving home in the middle of the night from a Saskatoon, Saskatchewan dog show. Briefly at about two in the morning he awoke from a dead sleep and howled to Tina Turner's "Simply the Best". As many times as I played that afterwards, he never sang to it again, just the one time on a barren dark highway in the middle of the night with Blaze and I in the truck.

Many people asked me how I could live with Gunner after the aggression and I truly look at how many good times and fond memories we had. As rough as that time was, I often thought about humans and how we're all different in how we react to pain or illness. Many people will curl up under the blankets and just try to get better. Others will become quite crabby and miserable and even lash out at the ones they love.

In my mind, Gunner was the later, if he didn't feel well he was crabby and for me, I couldn't throw a dog away for that. Having said that, I also didn't have small children in the house and I could protect the other pack members from him. I have said before that the story may have been very different if I didn't have the support I did from the people around me or if I did in fact have children. I wouldn't have been able to afford taking the chance that others could be hurt.

I will say, knowing that Gunner became crabby while sick did concern me about what would happen as he got older. He had been very consistent in his life and when it came to illness or pain, he did lash out and aggressively. Tim and I would talk about this and together there was no way we could see doing anything other than enjoying the precious time we had with Gunner.

Tim and I discussed that we would just have to pray and see where God would take us. Together, Tim and I would face whatever came our way with the dogs and life in general and we trusted in each other that we were in it for the long haul and would work it out as a team.

Gunner – April 14th, 2014 – 7 years, 3 months old

22 ~ SNOW BLOWING

The Doberman is well known for being a high energy dog that like most large breeds requires a lot of exercise. This can be a difficult dog to have in Manitoba, particularly with our very long, cold winters which typically have large amounts of snow fall. In turn, the Dobermans have very short coats which leads to little protection to the cold elements. The Dobermans like other breeds with cropped ears also run a higher risk of frost bite on the tips of their ears due to circulation issues.

If one wants a Doberman without the high price of a purchase from a breeder, they just have to look at the online ads starting in December for free Dobermans to good homes. I think this is because the elements in Manitoba don't provide for enough outside activities for the Dobermans. They in turn, start getting into trouble in their new homes because of the excess energy they have.

Let's face facts, you wouldn't want to spend much time outside if you were half naked would you? The truth about Manitoba is that most of us humans do go into somewhat of a hibernation because it gets plain old damn cold! To put things into perspective for readers in warmer climates, we have to plug in our vehicles or they won't start. People have literally frozen to death in our climate. The plus side of it is, crime drops off in the winter simply because even criminals don't feel like going out!

Having said that, my family has always participated in winter sports as many families do. We dress up, load up and head out ice fishing even on the days with extreme weather warnings. To us, winter is an exciting time as we load up the Avalanche with our fishing gear and drive out onto the ice of Lake Winnipeg. We pitch tents and fire up our propane heaters in the hopes of catching the Master Angler Green Back Walleye!

Quickly after getting Gunner, he displayed a complete and utter lack of interest in snow or cold temperatures. I used to laugh at Gunner because every first snow fall of the year, he would refuse to go outside to go potty. He wouldn't have a "boo boo" in the house, but he'd hold it!

You could tell by the look on his face that he was seriously planning on holding it until the snow was gone. In Manitoba though, when the snow comes, which is typically in late October, it stays well into March. "Holding it" isn't an option for that length of time, but every year Gunner would try and the longest he made it was three days before he had to venture bravely out.

I learned very quickly to have a lot of inside activities for the dogs which was very difficult due to the small size of the house on Calder. What I would do though was, as the snow fell, I would consistently snow blow a large path all the way around the large yard as there were some days when it warmed up enough that the dogs could frolic outside.

Before Tim's arrival, snow blowing was a problem for Gunner. He was very used to being with me so didn't take well to being in the house when I was outside. At the same time, there wasn't enough bundling in the world that I could do for Gunner so he could be outside with me.

The first few times, I left Gunner in his kennel while I snow-blowed only to come inside after I was done to find his blankets torn up. Gunner rarely tore up his kennel blankets and only did so in a fit of anger. Besides the destruction, you could tell he was incredibly worked up as he would even vomit.

My next few attempts were to leave Gunner loose in the house where he could watch me from the window. This worked better but I'd often return to the house to find that he'd left his displeasure as a pile of poop dead centre on the living room carpet. He'd then ignore me for hours with his pissed off attitude. I never called these deposits on the carpet "accidents" because they weren't. I called them "on purposes"! Gunner was mad and letting me know in no uncertain terms!

Finally Gunner and I came to the understanding that if I was to do the snow blowing, the least I could do was let him watch from the warmth of the running truck. The amount of gas I went through in the winter months running the truck so Gunner could "supervise" was astronomical but he never damaged anything or pooped in the truck. In fact, he was happy as a lark doing this and so that's the way it went for years.

The first winter came for Tim and I and snow blowing was now different as Tim took it on in full capacity which I so greatly appreciated. Calder had a huge driveway that took one or two hours to snow blow just by itself. Tim then would snow blow the potty area for the dogs and their convenience which added on another good half hour of snow blowing.

Gunner always kept a close eye on Tim from the window and never pooped on the carpet because I was in the house to see it. The best part was, I didn't have to bundle up like the abominable snow man and do it myself!

Sadly for Tim, our first winter together was also one of higher than normal snow fall so at least twice a week he was stuck outside doing this task. Because of the driveway and potty area being such a huge task by themselves, I never did mention to Tim that first winter that I actually also did the inside perimeter of the yard for the dogs. I was quite certain that if I had, this may have caused Tim to pack his belongings! Who in their right mind would spend hours outside snow blowing the drive way, the potty area and then to boot, a race track of sorts that may never be used by dogs that hated going outside in the cold?

The Manitoba winter dragged on as it normally does and Tim played hours of hide and go seek with Gunner trying to burn off at least some of his energy. In the meantime, while Tim did this, he also bonded very closely to Gunner and really began to enjoy these games they played.

Gunner was special in so many ways! At the time of meeting Tim, I had finally gotten his hypothyroidism under control and monitored it very closely with more than the required testing. While we still had to have very significant rules to insure there were no aggression issues, Tim saw the kindness in Gunner and his natural loving side.

After Tim had moved into Calder in August of 2013, we soon had his son Trevor staying with us for visitation weekends. I can remember having concerns with Gunner and how to handle all this as I lived with the very strong memory of the "bad side" of Gunner. We had countless discussions with Trevor about Gunner and his issues. Fortunately though, Trevor was 14 and a very mature 14 at that, he understood the rules with Gunner and abided by them at all times.

I can truly say that we were back to living in harmony and Trevor fit perfectly into our home. The dogs all adored Trevor, particularly Blaze who consistently would sneak into his room, rummage through his suitcase and steal his socks. She wouldn't chew on them, she just held them and when Trevor would try to take them away, she'd very gently turn her head keeping his ball of socks just out of his reach.

I had mentioned that one thing I was always against was dogs mooching from the table while a family ate together. With Tim and Trevor though, the new habit of sharing food from the table with the dogs had become a regular occurrence which they both paid for dearly.

I always ate my meal in peace whereas Tim or Trevor constantly had drooling Dobermans with spit bubbles coming out of their cheeks staring at them intensely while they ate. I will say though that this was more than a fair trade for me. These dogs now were getting so much attention all the time by these two wonderful men that I welcomed a little bit of mooching.

The pack had never really experienced human food before as I never gave it to them. With Tim and Trevor sharing with them regularly, they opened up new worlds of fabulous tastes to the dogs.

Gunner proved to love all foods as did Blaze but Liar would go through flaming hoola hoops for celery or pineapple and soon enough, the dogs learned that not only did we eat the food, but we also prepared it which quickly lead to us having "sharks in the kitchen".

The minute the magic cold food box was opened, or as we humans call it, the fridge and meal preparation started, the sharks started circling, hoping food would be dropped. Liar soon got back into his counter surfing tradition as he realized that as a puppy, it was great to steal, now sometimes food was left out!

Sadly one of my birthday cakes had to be served with big paw prints on each side, a large hole eaten out of the centre, and the icing was riddled with nose prints. The Saran Wrap that had covered the cake showed up from Liar out in the yard a few days later.

Again, as you do in life, we adjusted.

The constant sound of "beep beep" would be heard in the kitchen as meals were made. Eating at the table was interrupted by loving but forceful nose nudges and the occasional whining which was always rewarded with little tidbits. The small kitchen was never cleaner though as nothing was safe from the "counter surfer" Liar.

Tim looks back and as close as he got spending so much time with Gunner while he was laid off from work that winter, Gunner stole a place in Tim's heart in one moment on an average day.

Tim, Trevor and I had come home from ice fishing and while we had a fabulous time, Tim was feeling a bit under the weather. Trevor had gone into the living room to watch television, Gunner was on out time with the other dogs in their kennels and I had started to make supper. Tim had gone upstairs to our bedroom to lay down for a bit as he wasn't feeling well.

As I started banging around in the kitchen making supper, Gunner made the fateful decision that impacted Tim to this day. Instead of mooching while I cooked, Gunner snuck upstairs and stood at the gate Tim had placed in the doorway to keep him out of the bedroom. Gunner slowly started whimpering at the gate with his famous squinty eyed smile, begging to be let in and Tim obliged.

At that point, Gunner jumped on the bed and snuggled real close to Tim realizing he wasn't feeling good and the two of them had a little nap together.

Tim has often brought this up as it was one of those moments that Gunner reached right in and touched his heart with love.

It's little things, moments in time that can impact us so deeply. In that moment on such a regular non eventful day, Gunner chose Tim over food, Trevor, myself, and everything else. In that moment, Gunner knew Tim needed him and he was there.

Trevor, Tim and I plugged through that winter the best we could by filling our weekends with dog time and ice fishing. We had our sad time with loosing Taxi but we understood as she was very old. While it was expected, it was still very difficult for us but we moved forward with focusing on the positive and remembering the fond times with her.

Just as most Manitoba people thought our winter would never end, the days started getting longer with more and more sunshine every day. That winter had stayed pretty cold and for the most part we saw absolutely no thawing well into March and even then the melting was minimal.

The daily temperature in April had started to get a lot warmer and the snow had begun to melt away but it was a very slow go. The Calder property was so nicely private because of all the wonderful mature trees circling the yard. But because of these trees, it prevented the sun from hitting a lot of the snow in the yard. There was an area at the back end of the yard that was now exposing beautiful green grass but to get there, you had to plow through two feet of snow drifts.

April 14, 2014, the house awoke to a beautiful warm sunny day, one of those mornings that you just know you have to spend outside. Both Tim and I agreed that this was the perfect Doberman day to get them out and blow off all their energy!

Trevor had slept over for the weekend and we had recently purchased him a used motorbike. As we all sat eating the wonderful waffles that Tim had made for us, we decided that Tim and Trev would spend the morning getting Trev's bike cleaned up and ready for the season. I, in turn had asked Tim to get the snow blower out for me as I'd do a path for the dogs over to the grass and around the yard.

When we finished our warm breakfast, the two men headed out and while I cleaned up the dishes, Tim got the snow blower ready for me. As they proceeded to work on Trev's bike in the garage, I set out doing the path for the dogs. I had decided that it was warm enough for Gunner to come out and "help" me for a little bit as he knew what the path meant so I knew he'd be excited.

As I pushed the snow blower through the yard, Gunner would nip my snow pants as if pushing me to go faster. He wouldn't jump through the snow as quite frankly he couldn't stand snow, but he did stay behind me nipping at me constantly.

Tim said he watched from the garage with Trevor and they couldn't stop laughing as it was obvious what Gunner was doing.

I carried on and persevered and finally had cleared a path to that grass patch by the back of the yard. The clearing was quite large as it followed the tree line across the yard and grass was visible the full length. The minute I reached the clearing, Gunner sprang onto the grass and started having what I always referred to as his "Doberman

Zoomies" where he sprinted back and forth with zero purpose other than running as fast as he could.

It was so beautiful to watch him! I turned off the snow blower just simply to take it all in. After a short time though, I had to get Tim. Gunner had become his boy too and I knew that Tim would enjoy watching Gunner in this moment!

I went to the garage with Gunner in tow and asked Tim to take a break and come see his boy play. Tim eagerly wiped the bike grease off his hands and with a smile followed me back across the driveway and into the yard.

Gunner was so excited that Tim joined us that he now started his zoomies again back and forth down the path and around the grass area. Soon Tim and I reached the grass area with Gunner, and Tim started a quick game of tag. In no time, this lead to me getting on the tree swing and as I went back and forth, Gunner would jump at me, at times even pushing me higher.

Tim and I traded places and soon, Gunner was pushing Tim on the swing and we were all laughing. Quite frankly, it looked absolutely ridiculous and yet fabulous at the same time. Who would think that a Doberman would push a human on a swing!

It's days like that when you think back to when you were alone as a single person and you had no one to share it with. Now, in that beautiful moment, I had the dogs of my dreams and the man of my dreams to share it with and a fabulous step son as well! The peace was absolutely amazing. I felt "full" inside, complete if you will and truly so blessed.

As I sit here writing this, I remember so vividly watching Gunner push Tim, and Tim laughing so hard. I remember that I had the biggest happy tears on my cheeks watching them together. This was everything I had ever wanted for and prayed so many times for.

And then it changed.

Gunner ran from the swing and I thought he was going around the corner of the snow pile to run up the path in one of his zoomies but instead he fell. I thought that maybe he'd slipped but as he laid there, both Tim and I noticed that he'd started having what seemed to be a seizure.

Tim jumped off the tree swing and we both ran to Gunners side as quickly as we could with shear panic in our hearts. As the seizure stopped, we noticed that Gunner wasn't breathing. Tim immediately started mouth to snout breathing while I gave compressions but we got no reaction from Gunner. While we both cried, we continued working on Gunner for what seemed an eternity but he never came back to us. He was gone.

Tim and I stayed on the grass kneeling over Gunner crying and holding each other in dis-belief it had all happened so fast!

I don't know how much time passed, but Tim gently picked our boy up and cradled him tightly in his arms and slowly carried him out of the yard and placed him in the back of the Escape. There was no trip to the vet to be had, our Gunner was gone from us.

Trevor joined us at the truck and as we looked at our boy in the back of the Escape we all cried together. We were so in shock, in so much pain but oddly it was a peaceful moment and still a beautiful day.

I called one of the Manitoba's pet crematoriums and together, we all took Gunner there. We picked out the urn for our boy and left his body there wrapped in one of his favorite blankets so he wouldn't be cold anymore.

I don't know how Tim drove us home that day as he was truly as devastated as I was. Our ride home felt so lonely without Gunner sitting in the back, propped up on the arm rest and shoulder checking for us. Gunner wasn't in the back trying to open the windows on us or whining because we had the child locks on.

Instead, we all sat quietly and for Tim and I, while we made no sounds, the tears just streamed down our faces constantly.

Gunner – Our Heart Dog

23 ~ OUR HEART DOG

On the beautiful early spring morning of Sunday, April 14, 2014, Tim and I shared the tragic deep loss of our boy Gunner.

There were no signs, no warnings, absolutely no indicators that this would happen to us but it did and we had to live through it. We found comfort in each other and often cried in each other's arms. We both now had this huge gaping hole in our hearts that seemed like it never would heal.

Tim had difficulties with this as he'd never felt this kind of loss of a dog before. It consumed him at times and literally brought him to his knees and when it did, I helped him up and when it did the same to me, he lifted me up.

He had difficulties talking to me sometimes because if he felt that bad only knowing Gunner for the short time that he did, then how much hurt must I have been feeling knowing Gunner from a puppy. But this wasn't the case, we both had developed a very deep bond with Gunner and I knew Tim's grief was as strong as mine.

I explained to Tim about the "heart dog" phenomenon and where I had more history with Gunner, it was obvious to me that Gunner was clearly a "Heart Dog" to both of us. We were so blessed to have had all the time we did with our Gunner and it was truly an honor to have him in our home. Not many people get or take that opportunity to know a dog as we did Gunner and it was a blessing even in our grief.

Hearing the alarm go off on Monday morning was difficult as both Tim and I waited in bed so hopeful that Gunner would start to howl us awake as he had so many other mornings. But Gunner wasn't with us anymore. His kennel, filled with all his blankets and quilts was empty beside us.

People experience grief in different ways. Many shut down altogether or avoid discussions that bring up memories to work through their grief. Tim and I, found that talking about Gunner and crying helped and we did a lot of that. We shared our memories constantly and where at first we'd laugh, we'd soon be holding each other and crying together. It takes time for that grief to heal and to realize that while they're no longer with us, a piece of them never does leave you.

Calder had so many reminders of Gunner, but Tim and I agreed that we'd take things slow and deal with things when we were both ready. Together, as a team, we'd work through whatever we faced ahead.

We both had difficulties going into that part of the yard where Gunner had passed so quickly. The images of Gunner falling to the ground remained in our heads for a long time but those images began to fade. It was very difficult for us to watch Liar and Blaze play in the yard as they ran, they jumped and played with such vigor just as our Gunner had. We worried that they too might just fall down on us and leave us as he had.

Tim and I never used that tree swing again but we did leave it there.

Slowly we began to see Gunner passing away on that day as being a blessing to us though. It may sound terrible, but when we discussed Gunner's passing it became obvious to us that he had in fact died so incredibly happy. He had us there beside him, the two people who he loved and who he knew loved him so much. We were all playing together, laughing, living and loving him! Most importantly, Gunner didn't suffer.

For a dog, or even a human, isn't that indeed the most perfect way to leave this life? So happy and loved, surrounded by your family and with no pain. I think many people pray for that.

I had kept in contact with many people from my various dog email lists and posted about Gunner's last day with us. The emails that were returned were of people sharing their sorrow and sending prayers that truly helped Tim and I in our grief.

People from all over Canada and the United States emailed, many of them saying how much they would miss hearing about how Gunner had come through so much with us. But more importantly, they voiced how much they appreciated hearing about Gunner's various problems. The stories I had shared made them fight for their dogs as well and trouble shoot medical issues that may not have been resolved otherwise. Particularly about the common mis-diagnosis of Hypothyroidism.

Sadly, we also got numerous emails from people who had put their dogs down particularly due to un explained aggression. After hearing about Gunner's problems, they had to wonder themselves, if their dogs had Hypothyroidism.

As the days went by, slowly we put the kennels away that were no longer needed to keep Blaze and Liar separate from our Gunner. That summer, we took down the large fence that created a barrier between the dogs out in the yard that dad had helped me put up years before. The metal cage that my cousin Johnny had welded for the Escape also was eventually retired as it was no longer required.

As we did all this, we realized just how many accommodations we had made for Gunner. Please understand, every one of those accommodations was so damn well worth it.

Where Tim had started playing his guitar multiple times a week, he stopped playing it for a number of months after we lost Gunner. Tim simply couldn't bear not having his Gunner sing "their" song with him. I saw him pick it up a few times and his tears would start. Tim would take a big deep breath, let out such a sad sigh and he'd put his guitar away again. I never pushed him though. I knew the day would come when he could play his guitar without Gunner but the time had to be right.

Eventually, Gunner's urn was placed beside the other urns of Isaac, Vegas and Taxi. As with Isaac, I eventually packed up some of Gunner's toys that he so cherished so no other dogs would touch them.

Lastly, Gunner's kennel beside our bed was taken down and a lovely nightstand that Trevor made in shops class for Father's Day was put in its place.

Our life changed dramatically for Tim and I that day, but we have moved on. We still talk about the fond memories of Gunner but we laugh more now and cry less.

We never had a necropsy performed on Gunner to find out why he passed away so quickly, but we didn't need to. I had done my research and knew in my heart that Gunner had finally succumbed to "Dilated Cardiomyopathy".

DCM is a very common occurrence in many breeds but particularly in Dobermans. To this day, good dog breeders are still trying to eliminate it from our canine friends with testing, diagnosis and careful breeding programs. DCM, though is a very difficult illness to eliminate due to the difficulties in diagnosing. Many times it's not even detected until the tragic loss is suffered.

I had kept in touch with Mandy who owned Gunner's father, Scorch and she like us, was heartbroken.

Scorch passed away as well at the young age of seven, but Mandy's vet had diagnosed his passing to be that of lung cancer. Mandy had always done heart monitors on all her dogs and had on Scorch many times but no heart issues had ever been indicated.

I often wonder if Gunner's life would have been longer had we diagnosed him earlier and medicated him appropriately for Hypothyroidism. It took me so long to find out, how much damage was done inside his body before his diagnosis without me knowing? I know in the end, that he died of DCM but I can't help but hold on to the fact that some of it is also my fault for not getting him diagnosed sooner.

But what about this! What if on that day with Michele, I had put Gunner down instead of neutering him? I am so thankful, as is Tim, that we had another three years of precious memories with Gunner! I never would have had the opportunity to watch him sing as Tim played guitar! Gunner never would have learned to shake a paw and he got so darned good at it!

Tim would never have experienced his first Heart Dog and for that Tim will always be so grateful. Gunner taught Tim about what dogs can give you. It's not something that I can type, or verbally explain but if you open yourself up to your dogs and give them the opportunity to teach you, they will give you something that no one else can!

A few months back from this writing, Mandy contacted me to let me know that Flare, Liar's mother had also passed away quickly and at the young age of seven with no indications of illness.

Flare was the daughter of Scorch. Mandy, upon Flare's passing, pulled all of Scorch's old medical files and x-rays and had them sent away to a specialist for analyzation. It was in that specialist's opinion that Scorch may have in fact passed away from DCM and not lung cancer as the previous vet had claimed. Having that knowledge now, It is possible that even though Mandy has always worked diligently with her testing, that DCM has now followed down through his bloodlines.

All we can do, all anyone can do, is take every day as a special one and enjoy it to our fullest capabilities. With our Blaze and Liar, we never know what tomorrow will bring and so we must treasure them today.

Whatever happens, Tim and I to this day still feel so blessed to have had Gunner. He was and always will be our heart dog!

Above : Blaze.
Below : Liar & Dolly (Tim's mom) surviving breast Cancer.

24 ~ TODAY, TOMORROW AND FOR ALWAYS

Yesterday, Wednesday, August 30, 2018, Tim called me in a panic on his way to work.

He was listening to the news and the head line story was of a family with a young child who was fighting a small town council for the life of their beloved pet. The mother had been walking the dog who is a Pitbull and the Pitbull had bitten someone. Town council rules stipulate that in a case like that, the dog is to be put down.

I could hear in Tim's voice the panic as he explained that this family had moved from Winnipeg into the small town because Winnipeg had banned the Pitbull breed. The family had actually packed up everything they owned and moved so as they could keep their dog because they loved her so much. Their dog wasn't "just a dog" or even "just a pet", this dog was their family member! Tim talked about how he never understood that before, how people could drop everything "just for a dog" but because of Gunner, now he "got it".

He asked me to call into the radio show and talk about all the different reasons, legitimate reasons for this possible dog bite incident. Tim wanted me to tell them about Gunner and all his problems. Maybe this dog was like Gunner and had Hypothyroidism but no one knew because they never did the tests. Maybe this dog simply needed two cheap pills a day to be well. Tim was legitimately concerned how their little girl will be so upset if she loses her best friend.

Last night in bed Tim asked me specifically to add some things to this book and I'll write them here for him.

He had a number of dogs growing up. Chimo was his beloved German Shepherd that Tim bought as an eight year old boy for $8.00, all the money he had in his pocket and that was a lot of money, especially for a young boy.

He also had another German Shepherd named King as well as a smaller scruffy dog named Chrissy.

These dogs were important to him and he spent a lot of time with his furry friends but he was raised differently, they were dogs. When he met Gunner and the rest of the pack, Gunner became his "family member" as did the other dogs in our home and it happened so naturally. Tim said with such conviction, "I really cared for those dogs, and I shared thoughts with them and they helped me when I was young, but Gunner was different!"

Tim admitted last night that he's scared. He's scared of the thought of losing Blaze as they are so incredibly close. She was his first real Doberman friend and he couldn't believe how on that first day they met that she snuggled him. It hurt so much to lose Gunner, he can't even bear the thought of losing his Little Miss Blaze. I could hear him getting choked up as he talked to me about it.

There have been a few times since Gunner has passed that Tim has been snuggling his Blaze and I'll see the tears well up in his eyes. We both still miss Gunner so, and would give anything to see those squinty eyes smiling at us and him so proudly shake his paw.

Where are we now?

Tim and I are doing very well together and are planning on getting married next summer. It's been over five years since that first day we met when I knew so strongly that he was the one.

He did continue to get laid off for the winters as happens in construction and while he was off, he and dad worked diligently on Calder preparing it for future sale. They did an amazing job on that home with a total, complete and full renovation of each and every room.

We found numerous houses on the water for us but the sales all for one reason or another fell through. It was difficult for us but we'd pick ourselves up and start house shopping again. At times Tim would get annoyed because as each house sale collapsed, through my tears I'd mutter, "Everything happens for a reason, we just don't know it yet. We'll find our house!" And we did!

In the fall of 2017, my mom and dad had decided it was their time, due to health reasons, to move from their house in Petersfield and into an apartment in Selkirk. After discussions, Tim and I realized the reason for the other house sales falling through and we purchased mom and dad's home. We're finally on the water!

Tim and I cried as we locked the doors for the last time on Calder. We put the key in the door and looked out into the yard, the yard that Gunner knew so well and the tears flowed freely.

As I sit here typing away on my laptop, Blaze is sleeping soundly and snoring like a chainsaw all curled up like a little deer beside me on her plush dog bed. She's ten years old now and doing really well but her muzzle is speckled with grey, she has her old age lumps and bumps and her eyes have that old cloudy shimmer in them.

Liar had his choice of snoozing on the couch or recliner chair by the living room window but he's specifically chosen to snuggle up in Tim's recliner today.

Liar just turned six this past March and still has piles of energy!

We have our beautiful country home on the water that we've always wanted. We go fishing now whenever we choose and while we sit on our dock, Liar and Blaze can play in the fenced yard a few feet away from us or lay on their deck with bones, but still see us.

We have a small fishing boat but we don't use it much because Liar and Blaze don't fit so well in it so we're keeping our eyes out for a Pontoon. It's funny, but Tim says Blaze specifically wants a pontoon so she can be "Queen Sheba" and bark at every one as we cruise the creek. I bet she would do that too!

Just like Calder, Liar and Blaze have their own bedroom across the hall from us. It has both their kennels in it as well as their loaded toy box and a snuggly carpet on the floor for them. The walls are covered in dog show ribbons and pictures of all the dogs loved and lost in the past. The best picture though is a large cross stitched picture that my cousin Johnny's wife Dawn made for me of Gunner. It took her weeks to finish and it's an amazing sight to see.

Even with this beautiful bedroom, Liar and Blaze barely spend time in it because they still always want to be in our five square feet. They of course go in there for supper times and bedtime but the rest of the time, they're with us.

After selling my Green Escape, we picked up another SUV and while it's a very nice vehicle, the seats don't fold down like they did in the Escape. Blaze has problems getting in and out of it because it sits higher, so we've decided to sell it and purchase mom and dad's old Escape. All because it would be better for Blaze and she does like her car rides.

Blaze has taken to chasing chipmunks and gets very close to them but they always manage to just barely slip through our fence. As she stares so intently at the fence, those damn chipmunks sneak back into the yard at the other side where she chases them yet again.

When we bought our new living room furniture, Tim specified that we pick Blaze up her own chaise lounge, which we did. It sits right in front of the living room window and has never been sat on because she chooses to sprawl out on the couch as it's far more comfortable and the view is the same.

Tim jokes with Blaze that they're NOT friends on a regular basis.

As Blaze continues to throw herself across Tim's body when he comes home from a long day at work and insists that he pat her, he says lovingly, "We're NOT friends. Alls' I ever wanted was a dog who kept my feet warm, got me my slippers and who got me the paper. You have never done any of those things! Instead, you get drool on my pillow, you always want pats, you always want my food and make me sit on the couch with you and I'm going to call the dog pound. See how many couches they have for those dogs. They don't hardly have any toys, and those dogs definitely don't eat four times a day or have their own kiddie pool in their back yard!"

"We're not friends!" He says this so softly squishing in his cheeks like someone does when they stare at a cute little baby. As he speaks to her, she groans and stretches out just a little more and takes it all in. She knows he adores her and she definitely adores him!

They're not friends. She's his heart dog and his best friend!

Liar is a different dog altogether than Blaze and he's my boy. He's scared of the ceiling fan, there's one picture that he's not fond of hanging on the wall and sometimes the one curtain moves when the window is open. He stares at them from time to time like Gunner used to stare at the vacuum cleaner and it warms my heart. Liar has always been a quiet, shy, gentle and sensitive boy, but we work with him and from time to time he surprises us with his courage.

Last year, when Tim's mom, Dolly and step dad, Jake came over to visit, Liar detected cancer in Dolly's left breast.

As we all sat around the kitchen table to play a game of dice, Liar got up, walked straight over to her and started poking her harshly in her breast with his nose. Liar always liked Dolly but usually he'd greet them and then lay down beside me. In this case he waited in his corner until she sat down and then he proceeded to go over to her and poke her. As many times as I told him to knock it off, he wouldn't.

It was an incredibly awkward moment as he'd never acted this way before! I actually had to get up and pull him over to me so as he would leave Dolly alone. I then proceeded to tell everyone about a story where a dog bit his owner's breast, actually drawing blood and at the hospital they had detected a lump while placing the stiches. That lump had been tested and proved to be cancerous.

I felt bad that night as I feared that maybe I scared Tim's mom and it turned out I had. The next day she booked an appointment with the doctor and sure enough they too also detected a very small lump. They got her in shortly thereafter for a biopsy that proved to be a very aggressive cancer and her breast was immediately removed.

Dolly brings Liar fortune cookies every time they come over now as he seems to have chosen them as his favorite treat. She comes into our home, Liar goes straight to her and sniffs where her breast used to be and then quickly lays down beside her almost as if he's saying, "All good, no cancer!"

So Liar has his things too, his "quirks". He's shy, quiet and can be downright skittish at times but he also detects cancer and saves lives.

I still talk to Mandy, Michele and Donna and of course am still very close with Aunty Dee and Uncle Dan.

Aunty Dee and my adopted Aunty Eileen have been hired to proof read this book for me and are excited about it. I don't know how honest they'll be because I'm quite sure they're biased but I offered to pay them in hugs and they accepted. Aunty Dee did say if this book makes millions we'll have to renegotiate the payment. We'll cross that bridge when we get to it!

My Aunty Shirley who adored that little fawn sister of Gunner's that day he picked me out, sadly passed away some time back and we miss her feistiness!

We're going over to mom and dad's apartment this weekend for supper and dad was here just a few days ago for some quality fishing time on the dock. Tim and I will be forever grateful for all the love and support they've given us over the years.

Donna's Wicca is doing well and of course still on her thyroid meds but getting old and having some issues. Donna talked last weekend about a new German Shepherd pup she's thinking about.

Michele still lives at her home a few minutes from Calder and every year I do her taxes for her as she says "she's an animal person and so not a numbers freak!"

Mandy still breeds the occasional litter of Doberman pups and shows them but also finds herself very busy raising two gorgeous little boys with her husband in North Dakota.

After Gunner passed, I pretty much disappeared from the Dog Show world and where I miss it and the people dearly, I also don't miss it. I tried going back without Gunner and showed Liar until he got his Canadian Championship but stopped soon after as it was too hard. Those people, as amazing as they are, they remind me so much of Gunner. I looked at those show rings and where I was happy to see them, it hurt my heart that I couldn't take Gunner in as he so enjoyed it!

Hypothyroidism is an easily treatable situation when diagnosed but when it's not, it can literally turn your life upside down. I will always test my dogs for this regularly and highly suggest that you do as well. Blaze tested low at around three years old and has been on supplements since that time. Liar on the other hand, tested low at eighteen months and has been supplemented since that time as well. Neither of them have ever showed aggression but neither of them showed any of the classic symptoms either!

For me, the last company that I was the Controller for was recently sold and moved hours away which lead me to being un-employed. Tim suggested that I take this time and write about Gunner to remember him.

This book started out as a "numbers freak's" little journal about a dog that changed her life in so many ways, but I hope it's turned out to be so much more.

I want to publish this book now. I want people to read about Gunner and maybe it will help just one more dog. Maybe someone will force their vet to do just a simple blood test. Maybe, after hearing about all our good times, someone will let their dog be more to them then "just a dog". If you've heard nothing in this book, hear this, if you let those canines truly into your heart, you will gain so much more.

Lastly, maybe there's a single person out there giving up on finding their soul mate. Tim and I are living proof that everything happens for reason and only when the time is exactly right! Be patient and have faith!

Tim and I have learned so much about so many things over the years together. Everything happens for a reason and for today, tomorrow and for always, we are all so truly blessed!

~ Karen Grzenda, September 2018

Printed in Great Britain
by Amazon